"Matt Queen is the most evangelistic person I know. Not only does he share his faith, but God has gifted him to evangelize with excellence and compassion. Many of us struggle to share our faith effectively. *Everyday Evangelism* will help you sense opportunities, give you more confidence, and help you share your faith with clarity. I recommend it to every believer."

THOMAS WHITE
President, Cedarville University

"Matt Queen's *Everyday Evangelism*, has, again, provided all we could ask for by way of encouragement and support to begin or continue in personal and collective gospel outreach. Queen captures the New Testament spirit of evangelistic practice, offering rich biblical content and practical insight on why and how to share the good news. If you are looking for personal encouragement or want to encourage others to share the good news, *Everyday Evangelism* is the best resource available."

MARK W. McCLOSKEY, PH.D.
Professor Emeritus of Ministry Leadership, Bethel University
Author of *Tell it Often–Tell it Well*

"Matt Queen has done a thorough revision of his classic book, *Everyday Evangelism*. It is clear, simple, applicable, and compelling. It will be a blessing to you and become an excellent tool to help others become everyday evangelists! I highly recommend and commend it to you!"

JIMMY DRAPER
President Emeritus, LifeWay Christian Resources

"My first interaction with *Everyday Evangelism* was required. As an assigned text for a seminary course on evangelism, I obviously couldn't denigrate it since its author would be grading my review of it! However, I've come to cherish this book over the years and continue to return to it for help when evangelizing on my own or when seeking help in equipping my church members to do the same. Evangelism doesn't have to be "hard" or even daunting, and it can even become a part of your daily life and rhythm if you take the time to put simple practices and tips from this book into practice."

DR. MATT HENSLEE
Lead Pastor, Plymouth Park Baptist Church

"Many excellent print resources exist today that encourage God's people in the discipline of evangelism, but few are as practical and encouraging as Matt Queen's book, *Everyday Evangelism*. As I have had the privilege of knowing Matt as a professor, personal mentor, colleague, and close friend for many years, I know that the contents of this book come from one who has given most of his life as a practitioner of the gospel. If you desire to grow more faithful to the task of personal evangelism, make sure to pick up this book and allow it to encourage you in the days ahead. May God continue to use this resource as a catalyst to raise up many more laborers to go into the plentiful harvest!"

DR. BRANDON KIESLING
Associate Pastor of Gospel Proclamation, FBC, O'Fallon, Missouri

"When it comes to personal and church evangelism, I know of no one more knowledgeable biblically or practically than Matt Queen. Here is a wonderfully written volume, by a man who practices what he writes, to encourage you and the church to be involved in the most important task of evangelism. Solidly biblical, immensely practical, and clearly written, this volume is a must read on this subject. Don't miss it! Highly recommended!"

DAVID L. ALLEN
Distinguished Professor of Practical Theology and Dean
Adrian Rogers Center for Biblical Preaching
Mid-America Baptist Theological Seminary

"Evangelism is the story of redemption, and if anyone can tell that story it is Matt Queen. His book, *Everyday Evangelism*, is already a classic now in its fifth printing. Matt, with great skill and ability, takes the fear out of personal evangelism. He replaces it with confident hope that should fill every believer and will enable you to share the gospel effectively."

MAC BRUNSON
Pastor, Valleydale Church

"Sometimes good things come in small packages. This is an apt description of Matt Queen's *Everyday Evangelism*. Readers are whisked right to the heart of the matter with this informative and inspiring work on sharing our faith frequently and faithfully without excuse. As an introduction to the vital subject of personal evangelism or a refresher for those thoroughly acquainted with this eternally important task,

Queen's volume should be processed and practiced by all who know Christ and desire to make Him known!"

BOBBY LEWIS
Senior Pastor, Grace Baptist Church

"Do you long for the passion, boldness, and confidence that filled early church disciples in proclaiming the gospel?

Jesus tells us: "Go into all the world and preach the gospel to all creation" (Mark 16:15) so that all people will know the eternal hope He offers through His crucifixion and resurrection. He also commands us to take on this vital work because He knows how much we need significance and purpose in our lives that fulfill us profoundly However, when we reach the point of sharing with others about His awesome gift of salvation, we can feel fearful and ill-equipped. Why? Too often, it is because the church has unwittingly framed success in evangelism in terms of memorized formulas, human talent, and sophisticated arguments.

Thankfully, in his inspiring and down-to-earth explanation of Jesus' Great Commission, Dr. Matt Queen demystifies the proclamation of the good news, helping us understand what it is really all about in terms that anyone can comprehend. He brings us back to Scripture—demonstrating that true evangelism is prayer-infused, Christ-focused, and Spirit-empowered. Queen also teaches us how to overcome our qualms and embrace the Source that emboldened the disciples, giving them the evangelistic confidence, fervor, and urgency that characterized their lives.

If you are looking for help understanding and obeying Christ's Great Commission in your own spiritual walk or you wish to assist others in doing so, *Everyday Evangelism* by Dr. Matt Queen is the book you need."

DR. J. B. ROSANIA
Director of Content, Charles Stanley Institute

"Evangelism has never been more necessary—or more urgent—than it is today. In *Everyday Evangelism*, Dr. Matt Queen issues a powerful, Spirit-empowered call to action that is both deeply rooted in Scripture and perfectly suited for the spiritual challenges of our day. With clarity and conviction, he dispels fear and hesitation, reminding believers that true confidence in sharing the gospel comes through reliance on God's Word, the power of the Holy Spirit, and a life anchored in prayer. This book not only reignites readers' passion for evangelism—it equips them with biblical truth, practical strategy, and everyday encouragement to obey the Great Commission with courage, compassion, and urgency. Dr. Queen makes it clear: sharing Jesus isn't just possible—it's essential."

KELLY RICH, MABC, MTS
Biblical Counselor

"Dr. Queen's *Everyday Evangelism* is the best resource available for training believers in effective gospel proclamation. Combining biblical exposition, theological rigor, and practical advice, Queen hits the proverbial nail on the head for evangelism training and strikes the perfect balance between academic and pragmatic writing. Further, this resource mirrors Queen's personal life as he exhibits an insatiable desire to share the gospel message with all around him while also working tirelessly to train others to do so.

You would be well-served to use this resource for personal encouragement, one-on-one training, small group discipleship, church-wide events, or pastor and church staff resourcing. I cannot provide a strong enough endorsement for Queen's *Everyday Evangelism* as I know it will encourage you to share the life changing message of the gospel of Jesus Christ. Our love for and desire to share the gospel should be the first priority in our lives as Christians and *Everyday Evangelism* is the perfect resource to move each of us toward the goal of Matthew 28:18-20."

DR. TRAVIS S. KERNS
Associational Missions Strategist, Three Rivers Baptist Association

"In his book, *Everyday Evangelism*, Matt Queen encourages beginners and engages experts. What impresses me the most about this book is that Queen didn't just write it, he lives it. These principals have been successfully applied around the world. *Everyday Evangelism* is a true game changer for how churches and Christians should evangelize."

JONATHAN (JOBAL) BALDWIN
Pastor, El Bethel Baptist Church

"One of the grace-gifts God gives His churches is the evangelist. It is not the job of the evangelist only to evangelize, but to equip the saints for the work of evangelism. You will not find a more genuine and gifted evangelist than Dr. Matt Queen. *Everyday Evangelism* gives the reader an opportunity to sit under the equipping of a genuine, God-gifted evangelist. You will be encouraged, equipped, and challenged in evangelism as you work through this excellent book."

TOMMY KIKER
Pastor, East Leesville Baptist Church

"God has used Dr. Matt Queen as a powerful voice in raising up new generations to share their faith. This volume you hold in your hand is a valuable tool to the equipping process as you couple these nuggets of truth with the power of the Holy Spirit in your own life and become one of Christ's own witnesses yourself."

O. S. HAWKINS
President Emeritus, GuideStone Financial Resources

"The Lord gives us the incredible opportunity to share the good news of the gospel wherever we go, but it can be such a challenge in our everyday lives. If this is your struggle, too, then *Everyday Evangelism* must be your next read. Allow the Lord to work through Dr. Queen's biblical teaching, personal experience, and abundant encouragement, and then go tell someone about Jesus!"

LAURA DAILY
Church Member, Lane Prairie Baptist Church

"Dr. Matt Queen is the real deal. I've been privileged not only to be familiar with his writing and teaching for years, but honored to see him engage people in quiet places with a loving presentation of the gospel. *Everyday Evangelism* is a great alternative to the sales presentation evangelism that makes all of us cringe, as well as the directionless lack of intention that keeps us from being purposeful in our daily lives. You'll be thankful after you read this book."

JONATHAN GOODMAN
Discipleship Pastor, Green Street Baptist Church

"In our day, many feel that the culture around us resists the message of the gospel, with no place more challenging in America than in

Hawaii, where I previously served. In *Everyday Evangelism*, Matt Queen biblically defines evangelism, moves through the myths and fears of sharing Christ, and delivers clear and encouraging guidance for intentional, evangelistic engagements. I have witnessed God use this incredible book in reshaping the culture of everyday evangelism across Hawaii and the Pacific, with amazing results!"

DR. CHRIS MARTIN
Director of Convention Strategies, U.S. Engagement
International Mission Board

"Matt Queen's book, *Everyday Evangelism*, is not only for seminary students and church leaders, but also for every Christian who follows the Lord Jesus Christ. This book is biblical, simple, and practical; and as such it inspires and encourages every reader to share the gospel with lost people intentionally. Dr. Queen is a truly compassionate and winsome evangelist. His genuine love for the lost and passion for evangelism are contagious. I am so grateful for his friendship, insights, and impact on my life preaching the gospel around the world, particularly as a missionary in Africa."

D. DAVID LEE
International Mission Board Missionary
Professor of Evangelism and Missiology
Biblical Baptist Seminary of Madagascar and
Centre Evangelique de Formation de l'Ocean Indien

"In a day when evangelism is ignored in many circles as the responsibility and privilege of all Christians, Dr. Matt Queen does an exceptional job of reclaiming the biblical mandate. I would strongly recommend *Everyday Evangelism* for all believers desiring to embrace the Great Commission fully!"

DAVID WHEELER
Professor of Evangelism, Liberty University

"Matt Queen is a truly genuine and winsome evangelist. I admire his gentle conversational approach in sharing the gospel. *Everyday*

Evangelism explains what the Lord has taught Brother Matt through his humble submission to the Bible and Christ's Great Commission. Its message is simple. It is practical. And it works. If you need encouragement in evangelism, this is the book for you. Please read it and ask God to help you put its principles into practice."

THOMAS P. JOHNSTON
Senior Professor of Evangelism, Midwestern Baptist Theological Seminary
(2015)

"I have had the pleasure of sitting in Dr. Queen's evangelism seminary course and have used his book, *Everyday Evangelism*, in a course I teach myself. The book is easy to read and understand, even by those without a theological background. His suggestions are practical and the book's message inspires. If you are searching for a primer on evangelism in your church or small group, this is the book for you."

JEREMY PARKS
Pastor and Instructor

EVERYDAY EVANGELISM

EVERYDAY EVANGELISM

MATT QUEEN

FOREWORD BY KEITH E. EITEL
MISSIONARY, MISSIOLOGIST, AND AUTHOR

UPDATED AND REVISED FIFTH EDITION

LCCN: 2025914742
ISBN: 979-8-9993468-0-3 (paperback)
ISBN: 979-8-9993468-1-0 (e-book)

Available in paperback and e-book.

First edition: 2014 by Seminary Hill Press
Second edition: 2015 by Seminary Hill Press
Third edition: 2019 by Seminary Hill Press
Fourth edition: 2023 by Seminary Hill Press

Cover production by Mark Oberkrom (*oberkromdesign.myportfolio.com*).

Interior design and typesetting by Leason (Tripper) Stiles.

In honor of my dear friend, Dr. Thomas White—
President of Cedarville University, Cedarville, Ohio.

In 2014 you envisioned what I did not: that a collection of my blog posts could become a book. From that vision Everyday Evangelism *was born.*

In 2025 you once again encouraged, inspired, and empowered me to revise and republish Everyday Evangelism, *breathing new life into its pages and renewing my own passion for the task.*

I hope that one day we will rejoice together in heaven over the multitude of saints who were equipped for evangelism and the throng of sinners who entered the Kingdom because of our shared labor in this work.

Strong and courageous to the end.

TABLE OF CONTENTS

Foreword   i

Preface to the Revised and Updated Fifth Edition   iii

Introduction   v

Chapter 1
        Toward an Understanding of Evangelism   1

Chapter 2
        Spiritually Ripened Fields   19

Chapter 3
        Is It Biblical to Pray for the Salvation of Unbelievers?   29

Chapter 4
        Soil-Speculative or Soul-Driven Evangelism?   37

Chapter 5
        Overcoming Fears in Evangelism   43

Chapter 6
        Finding Evangelistic Confidence   53

Chapter 7
        Common Approaches to Share the Gospel   61

Chapter 8
        Questioning Your Evangelism   71

Chapter 9
        *A Strategy to Reach the Homes in
        Your Community with the Gospel*   87

FOREWORD

It was dark—a quiet, early morning taxi ride to the airport as we departed Penang, Malaysia. Dr. Matt Queen and I were there visiting a Baptist seminary. During that ride, he eagerly joined me in sharing Christ with our Muslim driver, seizing even that brief opportunity to point someone toward the gospel.

I have known Matt Queen for many years—first as a student, later as a colleague, and always as a brother. From the beginning, he has been unwavering in his conviction that every person he encounters needs to hear the saving message of Jesus Christ and be lovingly invited to receive the eternal gift of salvation. Matt is, by God's design and calling, an evangelist—*every day*.

Not only does he live out this calling passionately, but he is also academically and professionally equipped to teach it, having earned a Ph.D. in Evangelism and formerly occupied the world's first and oldest academic chair of evangelism—Southwestern Seminary's "Chair of Fire." In *Everyday Evangelism*, Matt draws from this deep well of personal experience, biblical conviction, and scholarly training to guide readers into a lifestyle of faithful witness.

He begins by laying a strong theological foundation for understanding evangelism, then skillfully moves to practical application, addressing real questions and challenges that believers face. Matt reminds us that God is already at work, preparing hearts long before we speak. Our role is simply to obey—that is, to deliver the message—God alone does the saving.

For those who feel hesitant or fearful about sharing their faith, this book offers both practical wisdom and heartfelt encouragement. Matt helps readers see that the true burden is not in evangelizing, but in remaining silent. If we neglect personal evangelism, we must reckon with the uncomfortable truth that we are withholding the very hope people most need.

Let me offer a gentle warning: if you are content to remain disobedient to Christ's Great Commission, you may find this book unsettling. But if you approach it with an open mind and a willing heart, God will use it to transform your life. Your one life, when surrendered to Him, can make an eternal difference for the advancement of His Kingdom.

KEITH E. EITEL, D.Theol., D.Miss.
Retired Dean of the Roy J. Fish School of Evangelism and
Missions, Southwestern Baptist Theological Seminary

PREFACE TO THE REVISED AND UPDATED FIFTH EDITION

Outside of God's creative orchestration, *Everyday Evangelism* would never have been published. It originated from a series of blog posts I wrote for Southwestern Baptist Theological Seminary's faculty blog, *Theological Matters*. Initially my intentions were not to write a book; I desired only to cooperate with my faculty colleagues in writing essays that would encourage members of Southern Baptist congregations. However, as God would have it, then-vice president of the seminary, Thomas White, determined that, based on reader interest, my essays were encouraging churches and believers to practice intentional evangelism.

In 2014 the seminary compiled my blogposts, along with a few additional chapters I wrote, into an evangelism primer now known as *Everyday Evangelism*. Thank God for His plan, His providence, and His purpose in this book that almost was not, after four editions and now this updated and revised fifth edition! He also used it as the template for the volume I consider to be my most monumental manuscript on evangelism—*Recapturing Evangelism: A Biblical-Theological Approach*.

Two new features of this updated and revised edition include a "Personal Reflection Guide" and a "Group Leader Discussion Guide" at the end of each chapter. The "Personal Reflection Guide" provides ways for individuals to internalize and apply each chapter. The "Group Leader Discussion Guide" serves to facilitate group interaction and the implementation of each chapter's principles in the local church.

Everyday Evangelism presents biblically-driven, evangelistic themes that motivate readers and their churches to make commitments to practice evangelism every day. However, readers should read this book with caution. It challenges some of today's most commonly accepted evangelism misnomers first by identifying how evangelism was practiced in the Scriptures and then by applying biblical principles to inform contemporary practices of evangelism.

Everyday Evangelism does not purport to be "the book" on evangelism. Instead, it seeks to convince readers that the Bible is "the Book" on evangelism. May the Lord use this book to enlist, equip, and encourage readers to practice biblical and intentional evangelism every day.

MATT QUEEN
Grace-Gifted Evangelist

INTRODUCTION

In 1950, the Southern Baptist Convention was comprised of 7,079,889 members. The 27,788 churches to which these members belonged reported 376,085 baptisms, meaning that one person was baptized for every nineteen members. In 2024, the Convention's 46,876 churches reported 12,722,266 members and 250,643 baptisms. The baptism-to-member ratio increased to one baptism for every fifty-one members—5,642,377 more members and 19,088 more churches resulted in fewer baptisms and a higher baptism-to-member ratio!

While certain factors, such as the increasing number of Southern Baptist churches that fail to report their Annual Church Profile (ACP)—that is, an annual statistical census reported by Southern Baptist congregations to Lifeway Christian Resources—explain some of this discrepancy, this higher baptism-to-member ratio identifies a glaring deficiency among Southern Baptist churches. The need of the hour in our churches is that we practice *everyday evangelism*. **Everyday evangelism** promotes a culture in which church members regularly share their faith in Christ as a natural part of their daily lives.

Motivating and mobilizing your church in *everyday evangelism* can be a daunting endeavor. Nevertheless, you have decided to read this book because you are up to the task! A simple strategy to assist you as you create a culture of *everyday evangelism* in your church includes the following:

1. PRAY

Seek the Lord's direction, power, and blessing for this evangelistic endeavor through prayer. Regardless of how well-intentioned and prepared the personal evangelist is, he needs the Lord's direction and wisdom in order to begin this endeavor and see it sustained in his church. Ask God to empower you in making evangelism contagious in your church. Involve your church members in regular times of focused prayer for the salvation of the lost in your community. Also, pray that the Lord will begin to stir a passion for consistent evangelism within your church members' hearts. Last, seek the blessing of God upon this endeavor. Apart from His blessing, any attempt to promote an *everyday evangelism* kind of atmosphere in your church will fail.

2. COMMIT

Make a personal commitment before God to practice intentional *everyday evangelism*. Ask God to help you keep this commitment. Share this commitment with others in your church, and ask them to encourage and keep you accountable to fulfill it. Consider your daily agenda, and intentionally schedule evangelism into your day.

3. ENCOURAGE

Invite others in your church to commit to daily, intentional evangelism. Not everyone you invite to become a consistent personal evangelist will make this commitment, but some fellow church members will commit if someone will only ask them. Periodically send those who make such commitments notes, emails, or text messages to encourage them and assure them you are praying for them as they evangelize.

4. EVANGELIZE

Ask those who make such commitments to accompany you during the church's scheduled evangelism outings. Keep in mind that some of those who commit are would-be personal evangelists, needing someone to teach them how to share the gospel. Share some basic gospel presentations with them (*e.g.*, *The Romans Road*; *Steps to Peace with God*; *One Verse Evangelism*) and encourage them to consider memorizing at least one such presentation. Demonstrate how to utilize the gospel presentation they select in live evangelism encounters. Also, invite them to begin to participate in the evangelistic conversations, assuring them that they can do so at their own pace and that you will assist them in the conversation if they experience any trouble.

Others who commit to evangelize have confidence in sharing the gospel but have never equipped someone else to evangelize. Encourage them to identify a few fellow church members to train in evangelism. Make yourself available to advise and counsel them whenever they have questions about the best training practices. Over time, also challenge them to teach those they have trained in evangelism how they, too, can equip and train future, would-be personal evangelists.

PERSONAL REFLECTION GUIDE

1. **What is your church's baptism-to-member ratio?**[1]
   » If you do not know, ask one of your church's pastors or its clerk to calculate the ratio for you.
   » Is it higher or lower than you expected?
   » What does the ratio suggest about the evangelistic involvement of the members of your church?

2. **What are some concerns relating to yours or your church's evangelism that need prayer?**
   » Identify someone in your church who will regularly pray with you about these requests; then ask for his commitment to join you.

3. **Who in your church can kindly hold you accountable to your evangelism goals?**
   » Make a list of some possible accountability partners who can encourage you to meet your goals, and then enlist one of them for the task.

---

1 Your church's baptism-to-member ratio is the total number of your church's members divided by the number of baptisms recorded over the past calendar year. This figure reflects how many members belong to the church for every one baptism recorded in the past year. For example, if a church has one hundred members and baptized five people, then one person was baptized for every twenty members.

You may be asking, what is the purpose of a church's bapism-to-membership ratio? A lower ratio (like 1:20) usually means more members are involved in evangelism, whereas a higher ratio (like 1:70) might show that only a few members are sharing their faith. The ratio is a helpful tool to indicate how well or poorly a church is fulling its mission to make baptized, obedient disciples through evangelism.

4. **Who are two or three church members you can invite to join you in consistently sharing the gospel?**
   » Make a list of some possible witnessing partners; then ask them if they are willing to participate with you.
5. **What simple gospel outline will you use when you evangelize?**
   » If you do not have one in mind, then ask a pastor in your church to suggest one to you, or choose one from the "Evangelize" section in this chapter.

GROUP LEADER DISCUSSION GUIDE

TOPIC	ENGAGE THE GROUP	EXPLORE THE ISSUE	EXECUTE THE PLAN
1: Our Church's Evangelistic Participation	• Have one of your pastors or the church clerk to calculate the baptism-to-member ratio of your church, then provide it or display it for the group. • Concerning it, ask the group, "Is our church's baptism-to-member ratio higher or lower than you expected?"	• Ask, "What does this ratio reveal about how active our church members are in sharing the gospel?"	• Ask, "What steps should we take to increase evangelistic participation?"

TOPIC	ENGAGE THE GROUP	EXPLORE THE ISSUE	EXECUTE THE PLAN
2: Evangelistic Prayer Needs	• Ask the group, "In what area(s) of evangelism do we need God's help the most? What about our church?" • Ask, "What is one thing we can ask God to do in and through our church to reach more people with the gospel?"	• Ask, "What evangelistic needs (*e.g.*, unreached groups; broken relationships; spiritual apathy) exist in our local community?" • Ask, "Who are some unbelievers for whose salvation we should pray?"	• Ask, "Would anyone like to volunteer to be a prayer partner with someone else in the group?" • Ask, "Who are others in our church that might commit to pray with us about these requests?" • Pray right now as a group for these needs.
3: Accountability for Evangelism	• Ask the group, "Why is accountability important in evangelism?" • Ask, "What does helpful and loving evangelistic accountability look like?"	• Ask, "What is a simple, realistic goal that each of us can set for sharing the gospel—such as sharing the gospel a certain number of times per day, week, or month, or starting a gospel conversation in specific situations (*e.g.*, asking someone wearing a cross, 'What does that cross mean to you?')?"	• Ask, "How can members of this group hold one another accountable to their personal evangelism goals?"

TOPIC	ENGAGE THE GROUP	EXPLORE THE ISSUE	EXECUTE THE PLAN
4: Evangelizing with Fellow Church Members	• Ask the group, "How can evangelizing with others help each of us stay motivated and encouraged?"	• Ask, "What are some venues in which church evangelism teams could share the gospel (*e.g.*, door-to-door; a coffee shop; a soup kitchen)?"	• Ask, "Would anyone like to partner with others in this group to begin evangelizing together?" • Ask, "Who are two or three church members that each group member could ask to join him to evangelize regularly?"
5: Knowing What You Will Share	• Ask the group, "Would anyone like to share a simple gospel outline they know?"	• Ask, "What key elements must be included when sharing the gospel (*e.g.*, sin; Jesus' death/burial/resurrection; a call to repent and believe)?"	• Ask, "Who would like to share with the group the gospel outline he often uses when he evangelizes?" • Practice sharing the gospel in groups of two or three.

CHAPTER 1

TOWARD AN UNDERSTANDING OF EVANGELISM

Three telephone pole installation crews sought to win an installation contract with their local telephone company. The phone company decided that it would put all three crews to a test. Each team would be given one day to set as many telephone poles in the ground as possible.

When the day was over, the first crew reported to the phone company official that they had installed thirty-five poles in the ground. The company representative was very impressed! The second crew reported that they had mounted thirty-two poles in the ground. The phone official relayed to the second crew, "That's good, but it's not good enough." Finally, he asked the third crew: "How many poles did you set in the ground?" The foreman proudly announced, "Two!" "Two?" asked the phone company official. "Why are you so proud of installing only two telephone poles? This team set thirty-two poles, and the other team set thirty-five." "Well, yeah," said the foreman, "but look at how much they left sticking out of the ground!"

WHAT EVANGELISM IS NOT[1]

In the same way that the third crew misunderstood the task at hand, many would-be personal evangelists want to practice *everyday evangelism*, but they misunderstand what *evangelism* is. In order to understand the meaning of *evangelism*, churches and believers first must understand what *evangelism* is not. Consider the following common misconceptions of *evangelism*:

1. Using Words When Necessary[2]

Some churches and believers think they practice evangelism on the basis of their moral and upright lifestyles apart from actually verbalizing the gospel. They believe the difference that Christ has made in their lives on its own merit, apart from a verbal declaration of the gospel, will itself raise unbelievers' curiosities and lead them to approach believers with their inquiries and interests in the gospel. Practitioners of this approach fondly assert a common misnomer attributed to Francis of Assisi: "Preach the gospel; use words when necessary."[3]

---

1 Authors of prominent textbooks and books on evangelism have identified general misconceptions about evangelism in order to define evangelism biblically. For examples, see George E. Sweazey, *Effective Evangelism: The Greatest Work in the World* (New York: Harper & Brothers, 1953), 21-22; C. E. Autrey, *Basic Evangelism* (Grand Rapids: Zondervan, 1959), 26-30; Mark Dever, *The Gospel and Personal Evangelism* (Wheaton, IL: Crossway, 2007), 69-82; and Dave Earley and David Wheeler, *Evangelism Is . . . : How to Share Jesus with Passion and Confidence* (Nashville: B&H Academic, 2010), vi-ix; Matt Queen, *Recapturing Evangelism: A Biblical-Theological Approach* (Brentwood: B&H Academic, 2023), 1-34, 275-284.

2 An expanded discussion of this misnomer is presented in Queen, *Recapturing Evangelism*, 11-14.

3 Mark Galli discredits this quote's being attributed to Francis in *Francis of Assisi and His World* (Downers Grove: InterVarsity, 2003). Also,

Tommy Kiker has retorted, "'Go, preach the gospel, use words when necessary,' is like saying, 'Go, feed the hungry, use food when necessary.'" Besides merely living moral and upright lives, believers have been called to live according to the highest standard of righteousness—that is, holiness (cf., Eph 1:4; 5:27; 1 Pet 1:15-16). While believers' lifestyles must match the demands of the gospel, believers must not forget that evangelism necessitates a verbal proclamation of the gospel. They, like first-century believers, are called to preach the gospel (cf., Acts 10:42; Rom 10:15; 1 Cor 1:17; Gal 1:15-16; Eph 3:8; and 2 Tim 4:1-2), not merely to live holy lives.

On this point, consider the model of the apostles and first-century believers. They do not "use words when necessary" when they practice evangelism in the New Testament. Words are necessary for personal evangelists in the New Testament! Examples of New Testament evangelism occur in the context of proclaiming the message of the gospel, not merely demonstrating the effects of the gospel. In fact, the New Testament addresses this kind of evangelistic approach only once, and in that case, it particularly refers to the marriage between a believing wife and an unbelieving husband (1 Pet 3:1-2). As such, this passage's specific context and intent are not prescriptive for all believers—that is, for the majority of Christian men and women for whom this situation does not apply; nor should it be adopted by all believers as a normative, evangelistic approach.

---

he states the following in a subsequent *Christianity Today* article: "This saying is carted out whenever someone wants to suggest that Christians talk about the gospel too much and live the gospel too little. Fair enough—that can be a problem. Much of the rhetorical power of the quotation comes from the assumption that Francis not only said it but lived it. The problem is that he did not say it. Nor did he live it." "Speak the Gospel, Use Deeds When Necessary;" accessed on May 8, 2014, *http://www.christianitytoday.com/ct/2009/may-web-only/120-42.0.html.*

2. A Job Only for Professionals[4]

This misconception of evangelism advances a narrative that only certain people can, or should, evangelize. A number of churches and believers consider evangelism to be a task only for professionals, that is—pastors, preachers, and evangelists. They are convinced that only those with "the gift of evangelism" have the ability and the responsibility to evangelize.

This mindset fails for many reasons. First, the Bible never mentions "a gift of evangelism." However, Paul does identify "the gift of the evangelist" (Eph 4:11). He explains that the spiritual (literally, the grace) gift of the evangelist is not some special ability he has been given to evangelize better than all the other saints; rather, it is a supernatural ability he has been given to equip all the saints to evangelize (Eph 4:12-13). Second, the evangelistic enterprise of Christ's kingdom cannot advance by means of evangelism practiced only by evangelists while every other believer stands by evangelistically idle because God has ordained that *all* believers evangelize. Nowhere in the Gospels does our Lord appoint only spiritually gifted evangelists to fulfill the Great Commission on their own. If He had, not all of those first disciples who received the Great Commission would have evangelized others or encouraged the disciples they made to evangelize; but they did! Last, if the task of world evangelization falls only upon spiritually gifted evangelists, then Jesus' promise to be with us always (Matt 28:20) would apply only to personal evangelists.

---

4 An expanded discussion of this misnomer is presented in Queen, *Recapturing Evangelism*, 5-11.

3. Anything and Everything You Do for God[5]

Many Christians embody the prevailing sentiment that any and every activity that occurs in their churches constitutes evangelism. While churches and believers should do everything they do with an eye toward evangelizing, the sad reality is that they do not. Because churches and believers do lots of different kinds of things, they convince themselves that their activities constitute evangelism even if they have not shared the gospel in the course of all they are doing. Thus, they believe when they host a pot luck meal and many unbelievers attend, they have evangelized. Some have convinced themselves that because many guests visit their church on a particular Sunday morning, evangelism has occurred. Still yet others think they have evangelized on the basis that they have offered a ministry (*e.g.*, Vacation Bible School; a financial workshop; a marriage enrichment weekend; a food pantry; a clothes closet) to the community. While all of these endeavors and situations are commendable and can be outlets to evangelize, those who think anything and everything they do is evangelism must realize that if the gospel of Jesus Christ is not verbally proclaimed and offered to those in attendance, then an event, not evangelism, has taken place.

4. Something You Do When You Get Time[6]

Some believers tell themselves they will evangelize when they feel like it or have the time to do so. This mindset inevitably relegates evangelism to a pastime activity, if it even occurs at all. In

---

5 An expanded discussion of this misnomer is presented in Queen, *Recapturing Evangelism*, 278-279.

6 An expanded discussion of this misnomer is presented in Queen, *Recapturing Evangelism*, 14-19.

order for *everyday evangelism* to take place, it must be intentional and sometimes even planned. Those who fail to plan time to evangelize will fail to find time to evangelize.

5. Telling Someone, "You are One of God's Children"[7]

Either telling others they are already God's children, or simply believing it to be true, constitutes a "everyone is good with God" kind of misconception about evangelism. One specific example of this approach can be found in Steve Smith's and Ying Kai's book, *T4T: A Discipleship Re-Revolution*. In it, Smith says that Kai began evangelistic conversations by stating, "Congratulations, you are God's child! The problem is that you are lost, but I will show you how to be saved."[8]

The Bible teaches that all people are God's creation (*cf.*, Gen 1:27), but only repentance of sin and faith in Jesus Christ alone appropriates men and women as the children of God (*cf.*, John 1:12; Rom 8:16; 9:7-9; and 1 John 3:1). If we tell our hearers that they are God's children already, then why would they want to repent and believe? In fact, taking this statement to its logical conclusions can promote a type of "Christian" universalism that assumes everyone will be saved in the end. Everyday personal evangelists are not spiritual gurus; they are God's mouthpieces that sound forth God's love for the world through Jesus Christ's death, burial, and resurrection and call for everyone everywhere to repent of their sins and believe in Jesus Christ alone for salvation.

---

7 An expanded discussion of this misnomer is presented in Queen, *Recapturing Evangelism*, 19-22.

8 Steve Smith with Ying Kai, *T4T: A Discipleship Re-Revolution* (Monument: WIGTake Resources, 2011), 217.

6. Shaming Others[9]

Personal evangelists, who on their own authority and/or for their own pleasure condemn and shame others during an evangelistic encounter exemplify the "shaming others" mentality. In this approach, personal evangelists seek to make listeners feel bad about themselves apart from the conviction of the Holy Spirit. Extreme cases of this attitude include so-called "personal evangelists" berating others without either talking to them or sharing the gospel with them.

Everyday personal evangelists must convey to their listeners that every sinner is judged because they have not believed in Jesus Christ (John 3:18-19, 36). Additionally, they must not neglect to tell those who continue to listen that Jesus Christ died on the cross for their sins, and if they will repent of their sins and believe in Jesus Christ, then they can be forgiven and declared righteous through Him. Likewise, sinners must be told that hell awaits them if they do not believe and repent, but everyday personal evangelists must tell them in such a way that their listeners realize that the evangelists care for their souls and want them to avoid hell through Jesus Christ and Him alone.

7. Winning at All Costs[10]

Some believers seem more interested in winning arguments than they do winning souls. In their well-meaning attempts to explain and defend the gospel, such Christians argue their point in hopes that their listeners will concede that the everyday personal

---

9 An expanded discussion of this misnomer is presented in Queen, *Recapturing Evangelism*, 22-24.

10 An expanded discussion of this misnomer is presented in Queen, *Recapturing Evangelism*, 25-29.

evangelist is correct and that they are wrong. The apostle Paul states five times in 1 Corinthians 9:19-23 that he has done everything he can do under the law of Christ to win others. By "win," neither does he mean simply to convince them nor to triumph over them. Rather, he intends to "win" them in the sense that he endeavors to lead them to faith in Christ alone (1 Cor 9:22b). Therefore, everyday personal evangelists should share the gospel with complete confidence in its veracity but do so for the reason Christ evangelized—so that people will repent and believe the gospel (Mark 1:15).

8. "Sheep Stealing"[11]

Other well-meaning church members encourage a member from another church to unite with their church and call what they do "evangelism," when in reality they exercise "sheep stealing." This practice proves unhealthy and essentially becomes a kind of "spiritual cannibalism." Although every church should promote an inviting and accepting atmosphere for believers who are searching for a church to which they can belong, this characteristic on its own merits does not constitute evangelism.

Churches and believers do not evangelize believers; they evangelize unbelievers. Furthermore, evangelism is not inviting already established believers to become members of a church (though such an invitation is encouraged if personal evangelists interact with believers who are not actively involved in a God-fearing, Bible-believing church). Rather, evangelism is inviting unbelievers to respond to the good news of Jesus Christ through repentance and faith by becoming His disciples, professing their newfound faith through believer's baptism, and

---

11 An expanded discussion of this misnomer is presented in Queen, *Recapturing Evangelism*, 279-281.

being taught obedience to all the commands of Christ (primarily by the local church into which they will be baptized and to which they will belong).

9. Merely Inviting Unbelievers to Church[12]

Some Christians simply invite unbelievers to attend their churches. While church members should invite unbelievers to their churches, any invitation to attend church that does not also invite them to receive Christ cannot be considered evangelism. What about lost people who never accept the invitation to attend a worship service in order to hear the gospel? Or, what about sinners who intend to come to church but suddenly die before Sunday comes? What if they do attend church, but the preacher does not preach the gospel to them? In order to evangelize unbelievers, everyday personal evangelists must present enough of the gospel to them so they know the reason why Jesus died for them on the cross, as well as the divine implications of His resurrection, so they might repent of their sins and receive Christ as their Lord and Savior through faith.

10. Seeking Credit for Saving Souls[13]

"Belt-notching" is a popular idiom that refers to those who boast of some success or achievement for the purpose of bringing attention to themselves. Believers who concern themselves only with "adding another notch in their belts" act out of pride in order to receive recognition for those who, upon hearing the

---

12 An expanded discussion of this misnomer is presented in Queen, *Recapturing Evangelism*, 282.

13 An expanded discussion of this misnomer is presented in Queen, *Recapturing Evangelism*, 32-33.

gospel, profess faith in Jesus Christ. Scripture exhorts personal evangelists not to boast or seek credit for what God does in the gospel through their evangelism (*cf.*, 1 Cor 1:31; 9:16; 2 Cor 10:12-18; Gal 5:25-26; 6:13-15).

11. Manipulation[14]

Unfortunately, some who intend to practice evangelism attempt to manipulate and pressure their hearers into making professions of faith. Those who use manipulation willingly abandon the convicting work of the Holy Spirit and attempt to force their hearers into a decision for which the Spirit of God has not prepared their hearts. Those who practice such things would do well to keep in mind that if they can talk people into making a decision, then others can talk them into making a completely opposite decision. Worse yet, manipulators can foster a false assurance of salvation within those who have not actually repented and believed in Christ, if not altogether harden sinners to receive the gospel because they believe they are saved when in reality they are not.

WHAT EVANGELISM IS

With so many misconceptions abounding, what, then, is *evangelism*? Any church or believer who endeavors to practice consistent everyday evangelism must understand the meaning of *evangelism*. ***Evangelism is that Spirit-empowered activity whereby all disciples of Jesus Christ should present an intentional, complete, and verbal witness of His life, death, burial, and resurrection to***

---

14 An expanded discussion of this misnomer is presented in Queen, *Recapturing Evangelism*, 33-34.

unbelievers, exhorting them to repent of their sins and place their faith in Christ alone for salvation so that they may become His baptized, obedient disciples. Evangelism aims that those who hear the gospel and become disciples of Jesus Christ will naturally and quickly become members of a local New Testament church of the Lord Jesus Christ through believer's baptism in the name of the Father, the Son, and the Spirit. Additionally, their local church body should both teach and hold them accountable to obey all of Christ's commands.

WHAT IS A SIMPLE EVANGELISTIC APPROACH?

Having identified the most common misnomers concerning evangelism, as well as defining *evangelism* and its aim, does a simple evangelistic approach exist that can assist believers in practicing everyday evangelism? Intentionality in evangelism is not simply knowing that believers should evangelize; rather, it is making a plan to evangelize consistently and then executing it. Any strategy that encourages believers to evangelize daily will result in everyday evangelism. One simple approach that expectant, everyday personal evangelists can utilize in their intentional efforts to evangelize unbelievers includes the suggested six steps:

1. Pray

Everyday personal evangelists who do not pray will find their evangelism meeting with failure. During their quiet times, periodically during each day, and before they gather for planned times of evangelism, believers should pray for God's Spirit to precede their witness and to empower their witness for Jesus with boldness. Praying for these requests guarantees neither that everyone who hears the gospel will respond in faith, nor that everyday personal evangelists can be assured they will not be subject to demonic interference. However, believers who fail to pray in preparation for their evangelism essentially forfeit the blessings of God and make themselves vulnerable to spiritual aggression.

2. Identify and Utilize Points of Contact

Personal evangelists will find no shortage of individuals who need to hear the gospel; however, those finding trouble identifying those with whom they will share the gospel will want to utilize daily points of contact. They can find points of contact beginning with those with whom they have previously established relationships (*e.g.*, unbelieving family; friends; neighbors). In addition, they can approach people like their barber/hair stylist, their dentist, or solicitors who visit their homes.

Some who desire to evangelize have determined to do so if God would provide them with obvious, divinely appointed opportunities; however, by "opportunities" they mean someone's approaching them and asking what they must do to be saved. Rarely, if ever, will these hopeful personal evangelists get these "opportunities;" therefore, consider evangelistic opportunities from God as those people with whom you come into contact, whose spiritual state is either unknown to you or obvious to you that they need Christ.

3. Articulate a Transition Statement

Once personal evangelists have identified points of contact for evangelism, they need to engage these people in conversation.

Because God is the creator of all things, personal evangelists should anticipate and listen for topics that arise in their conversations to transition to the gospel. Some examples of these transitions include the following: (1) discussing one's earthly father can be used to shift the conversation to explain how the Heavenly Father demonstrated His love by sending Jesus Christ to die for everyone's sins; (2) exchanging information about important life events can lead personal evangelists to share their testimony about how they came to faith in Christ; (3) hearing someone express fears relating to their impending death or concerns about their health can lead to a dialogue about how repentance from sins and belief in the gospel provides the only confident peace in this life and the next; and (4) being told the details of others' weekend activities can invite the opportunity for everyday personal evangelists to summarize last Sunday's sermon they heard and rearticulate the gospel invitation with which the preacher concluded his sermon.

4. Present the Gospel

Utilize any presentation of the gospel that is both biblically accurate and easy to remember. However, personal evangelists desiring to share the gospel in a more natural, extemporaneous way will want to ensure they present the core elements of the gospel. First, they must convey the reality and consequences of sin in the lives of their hearers. Second, they must declare the life, death, burial, and resurrection of Jesus Christ and how He alone serves as the provision for anyone to be reconciled to God. Finally, they must explain to their listeners that reconciliation with God through Jesus can only occur if they will repent of their sins and believe in Jesus Christ alone for salvation.

5. Encourage Questions for Clarification

After a personal evangelist gives a complete presentation of the gospel, he should ask his hearers the following questions: (1) "Do you understand what I have shared with you?" (2) "Do you have any questions about what I have shared with you?" and (3) "Have you ever made this kind of decision?"

If the person responds, "Yes," to the third question, then ask him to share with you when he made this decision and to provide some of the details of how he received Christ. If he testifies of having experienced biblical conversion, then encourage him to become an everyday personal evangelist if he is not already consistently evangelizing.

6. Invite Your Hearers to Receive Christ

If the person with whom you are sharing the gospel does not articulate a biblical conversion experience, then explain to him how his experience falls short according to Scripture, and invite him to receive Jesus through repentance and faith. However, if he responds, "No," then ask him if he will repent of his sins and believe in Jesus' death for his sins and His resurrection from the dead for his salvation.

Many of those who hear the gospel will decline to repent and believe. With complete sincerity, devoid of any manipulation, an everyday personal evangelist should advise anyone who declines the offer to receive Christ of the eternal consequences that accompany his decision and encourage him to reconsider. If he still rejects the offer of the gospel, then leave him with a faithful gospel tract that includes your contact information or the contact information of your local church.[15]

---

15 A personal evangelist can consider creating an email addres and

On the other hand, if the other person indicates that he would like to repent and believe, then summarize the gospel and emphasize the demands of the gospel. Ask him if he understands the decision he is about to make. Depending on his response, do the following:

1. If he indicates, under the conviction of the Holy Spirit, that he wants to repent and believe, then instruct him to call on the Lord for salvation (Rom 10:13) through repentance and faith. Remind him that Jesus, not his prayer, will save him and that he receives his salvation by calling on the name of the Lord in repentance and faith. Encourage him to express (1) his sinfulness before God; (2) his need for salvation through Jesus Christ alone; (3) his request for God to forgive his sins; and (4) his gratitude for God's grace to save him. If he indicates he needs assistance in praying, instruct him to pray the previous four aspects (pausing after each one to allow him to do so) in his own words, rather than having him repeat scripted words you give him.
2. If he previously misunderstood what he said he wanted to do but realizes he is not prepared to repent and believe, then encourage him to reconsider his response to the gospel, and leave with him a trustworthy gospel tract containing information whereby he can contact you or someone from your church.
3. If he says he understands the decision, but you are unsure whether or not he does, then reemphasize the high demands of the gospel. If he then becomes unsure about repenting and believing, follow-up with discern-

---

registering for a Google Voice number (*https://voice.google.com*). He can use the new email address and virtual phone number in lieu of his personal email address and phone number on the gospel tract. The new contact information will provide an intermediary step of security for the personal evangelist.

ing questions to determine how, or if, the Holy Spirit is working conviction in his heart that leads to repentance. If, however, upon hearing the high demands of the gospel and indicating he is being convicted by the Holy Spirit, he remains confident about his desire to repent and believe, then do not prevent him from calling on the Lord for salvation.

PERSONAL REFLECTION GUIDE

1. **Did any of the common misconceptions about *evangelism* in this chapter challenge what you have previously believed?**
    - » How has your concept of *evangelism* changed, if at all, after reading this chapter?
2. **How do you define *evangelism*?**
    - » How closely does this chapter's definition of *evangelism* match your own?
    - » What, if anything, is missing or included in this chapter's definition that you would change?
3. **Did you find the step-by-step proposal on how to evangelize helpful? Why or why not?**
    - » Which step(s) in the process was (were) most useful to you?
    - » Which step(s), if any, would you like to explore further or practice with another believer?

GROUP LEADER DISCUSSION GUIDE

TOPIC	ENGAGE THE GROUP	EXPLORE THE ISSUE	EXECUTE THE PLAN
1: Misconceptions about Evangelism	• Ask the group, "Which of your previous beliefs about evangelism were challenged by the common misconceptions presented in this chapter?"	• Ask, "How, if at all, has your understanding of evangelism changed after reading this chapter?"	• Ask, "Who would like to share with the group an evangelism misconception that has previously affected (or currently affects) the way you evangelize? How might this new understanding of evangelism change the way you will evangelize in the future?"
2: Defining Evangelism	• Instruct the group to collaborate together and formulate a definition of *evangelism*.	• Ask, "How closely does our group's *evangelism* definition align with the one in this chapter?" • Ask, "What, if anything, would we add or remove from this chapter's definition?"	• Have each member of the group compose his own definition of *evangelism* that takes into account this chapter and the group's discussion.

TOPIC	ENGAGE THE GROUP	EXPLORE THE ISSUE	EXECUTE THE PLAN
3: Adopting a Simple Way to Evangelize	• Instruct the group to collaborate together and formulate a step-by-step guide to evangelize.	• Ask, "Were there any steps presented in this chapter that the group's proposal omitted but should include, or vice versa?" • Ask, "Which steps, if any, would the group like to explore further or discuss how to practice in a real-life scenario?"	• Have each member select one step from either this chapter or the group's proposal to practice this week with a fellow small group member.

Chapter 2

Spiritually Ripened Fields

The *Harvest*—a short film that tells the real-life, inspiring story of a family on a North Dakota farm—opens with a father and his three young sons as they survey wheat fields that stretch as far as the eye can see.[1] The father explains to these would-be farmers, "By the end of the summer, the wheat will be ripened and the harvest will be ready to reap. When the harvest is ready, we must be ready, or we will lose the whole crop."

A few weeks later the father dies unexpectedly, leaving the looming harvest behind for his grieving wife and three boys. The oldest son remembers his dad's saying they would have to be ready when the harvest was ready or they would lose the entire crop. The burden of responsibility bears down on his shoulders, and he does not want to let his father's labors go to waste. He cannot lose the crop, but even the best efforts of both his brothers and himself will not be enough to prevent it from happening. Their everyday chores are more than enough work for them. The three boys pray

---

1 *The Harvest: A Modern Day Parable* is viewable at *https://vimeo.com/146853439.*

that God would send them help. With every day, the weather gets hotter, causing the wheat to ripen sooner than anyone expected. The day suddenly comes when the wheat is ready to be harvested, but the boys simply are not ready to reap it.

The oldest son wakes early in the morning, realizing the urgency of the task—how today is just one day closer to the day they will lose the harvest. After dressing, eating, and beginning his morning chores, he hears a growing roar and rumbling in the distance. As he looks, he can hardly believe his eyes. Huge combines, one after another, make their way into the harvest fields. It is as if the whole world has come to harvest the crop! Neighboring farmers begin harvesting the wheat in the big northern field until they finish the one in the south. Side by side, they move from field to field, leaving a path of the work they have finished behind them.

As the oldest son watches them unload the golden wheat, he remembers the prayers of him and his father asking for help with the harvest before his dad died. Then he understands—he was not alone. These people had work of their own, but they left their own fields to come and help his family. Together they did what no one could do on his own—they brought in an entire harvest in one day. The boys' prayers had been answered! The harvest was finished— the fields were clean—and the wheat was saved!

In the Gospels Jesus uses agricultural language, including a white, wheat-ripened field, to represent spiritual truths on various occasions. When sending out His disciples (Matt 9:37-38; Luke 10:2) and responding to His disciples' curiosity when He did not eat food they had brought him (John 4:34-38), our Lord directs their eyes to a ripened, white harvest of weary people ready to believe in Him. Laborers would be necessary in order to reap the spiritual harvest, so Jesus directs His followers in Matthew 9:37-38 and Luke 10:2 to pray that the Lord of the harvest would send them. In John 4:34-38, He commands them to reap the spiritually ripened field in which others had labored. In light of these passages, consider the following reflections concerning our Lord's commands and the spiritually ripened field composed of unbelievers.

The Spiritually Ripened Field Awaits Reaping

Jesus describes the "field" of unbelievers as both "abundant" (Matt 9:37-38; Luke 10:2) and "white" (John 4:34-38), indicating it is ripe and awaits reaping. In other words, Jesus tells His disciples that numerous unbelievers stand prepared to repent of their sins and to believe in Him. Although disciples who labor in a spiritually ripened field do not possess a guarantee to reap a harvest each time they work the field, they can be assured that (1) unbelievers across the globe are prepared to believe in Jesus as Lord and Savior right now and (2) their labors in the field sometimes prepare the crop for future ripening so that in due time others may be able reap it (cf., John 4:38). The work of the Spirit and the labors of past personal evangelists have resulted in today's spiritually ripened field, and today's evangelistic seed-casting cultivates a spiritually ripened field for the future.

Although we must prepare for future evangelistic endeavors, we also must remember that people are ready and willing right now to repent of their sins and believe in Jesus for salvation; however, they cannot do so apart from hearing the gospel proclaimed (Rom 10:14).

The Spiritually Ripened Field Demands Urgency

Jesus' description of the fields as "white for harvest" implies a demand for evangelistic urgency. Even an agricultural novice

21

understands that no particular field or crop remains ripened indefinitely. Christ's depiction of a whitened harvest reminds an evangelistic harvester that any conversation or encounter he has with an unbeliever potentially could be that person's last opportunity to respond to the gospel's call.

Laborers for the Lord of the harvest must not assume spiritually ripened unbelievers are independently or automatically reaped into the Lord's harvest. The notion that unbelievers obtain faith in Christ unconsciously or independent from a gospel witness is foreign to the Scriptures. In fact, immediately after Jesus identifies the fields as ready for reaping in John 4:35, John records, "Now many Samaritans from that town believed in [H]im because of what the woman said. ... Many more believed because of what [H]e said" (John 4:39a, 41). Note that the Samaritans' salvation did not occur solely on the basis that they were spiritually ripened. Rather, the numerous Samaritans who believed did so *after* hearing the testimony of the Samaritan woman and Jesus' word, not *automatically* on the basis of their own meritorious receptivity.

Because of life's brevity, unbelievers have limited time remaining to repent of their sins and believe the gospel. The spiritually ripened field will not be the same tomorrow as it is today. With every new day, evangelistic harvesters will observe certain field crops having been lost forever to death. Therefore, laborers for the Lord of the harvest must possess evangelistic urgency each hour of every day.

The Spiritually Ripened Field Receives Reapers through Prayer

In both Matthew 9:37-38 and Luke 10:2, Jesus instructs His disciples to pray to the Lord of the harvest for laborers. In particular,

Matthew precedes his account of this instruction by mentioning Jesus' deep compassion for helpless and harassed people. Instead of prompting anxiety concerning this overwhelming situation among His disciples, He instructs them to pray. Jesus informs His disciples that prayer-prompted harvesters are necessary in order for the plenteous fields to be reaped.

Our Lord leaves the work of His evangelistic enterprise neither to coincidence nor to convenience. In addition, He does not promote a strategy of lobbying, begging, or shaming others into evangelistic enlistment. Entrusting the reaping of spiritually ripened fields neither to chance nor to campaigns, the Lord of the harvest commands His disciples to pray for the mass deployment of evangelistic laborers to reap His harvest.

The Spiritually Ripened Field Requires More Than Prayer

Responsibility for harvesting the spiritually ripened field belongs to all disciples of Jesus. As previously mentioned, part of the responsibility believers assume is that of praying for the enlistment of harvest laborers. However, earnest intercession to the Lord of the harvest requires more than prayer alone. No one will ever pray for evangelistic laborers without also realizing his own urgent, evangelistic responsibility to join the endeavor.

No one ever needs to question whether a prayer to the Lord of the harvest for evangelistic laborers falls outside the rubric of God's will. Likewise, one never needs to doubt whether the Lord of the harvest will answer such a prayer. Inevitably, the Holy Spirit prompts us to become answers to our own prayers in this regard.

In a different context, perhaps you have heard someone remark, "Well, *all we can do* is pray." Usually someone responds this way when the situation or circumstance appears so overwhelming that he feels powerless to act. However, if a believer prays for evangelistic harvesters to be sent into the spiritually ripened field, he should expect to testify soon thereafter, "Prayer for laborers to enter the spiritually ripened field has prompted me to do *all I can do!*"

Conclusion

The Lottie Moon Christmas Offering for International Missions reminds most Southern Baptists of the global, spiritually ripened field when they are asked to give to support laborers. In his book, *Send the Light: Lottie Moon's Letters and Other Writings*, Keith Harper includes a letter Lottie Moon wrote on November 4, 1875, to the Foreign Mission Board (now the International Mission Board of the Southern Baptist Convention). In addition to the previous reflections concerning what the Scriptures teach about the spiritually ripened field, may we all consider and act upon Lottie Moon's plea to Southern Baptists of her day about today's spiritually ripened field requiring prayer-prompted harvesters:

> The harvest is plenteous, the laborers are few. ... What we find missionaries can do in the way of preaching the gospel even in the immediate neighborhood of this city is but as the thousandth part of a drop in the bucket compared with what should be done. I do not pretend to aver [claim] that there is any spiritual interest among the people. They literally "sit in darkness and in the shadow of death." The burden of our words to them is folly and sin of idol worship. We are but doing pioneer work, but breaking up the soil in which we believe others shall sow a bountiful crop. But, as in the natural soil, four or five laborers

cannot possibly cultivate a radius of twenty miles, so cannot we, a mission of five people, do more than make a beginning of what should be done. ... But is there no way to arouse the churches on this subject? We missionaries find it in our hearts to say to them in all humility, "Now then we are ambassadors for Christ; as though God did beseech you by us, we pray you, in Christ's stead," to remember the heathen. We implore you to send us help. Let not these heathen sink down into eternal death without one opportunity to hear that blessed gospel which is to you the source of all joy & comfort.[2]

Lottie Moon's words are as true today as the day she wrote them more than one hundred years ago. Though she is dead, she still speaks. Shall we who remain be stirred to enter the global mission field? Shall we sow gospel seed where she and others have broken the soil? Shall we reap the spiritually ripened crop? The Lord of the harvest awaits our urgent prayers for laborers, and He awaits our urgent, evangelistic labors.

PERSONAL REFLECTION GUIDE

1. **Is the Holy Spirit preparing unbelievers to respond to hearing the gospel just as much today as He did during Jesus' ministry?**
   » Do you believe that the Spirit is at work among some people groups and/or communities around the globe, making them more

---

2 Keith Harper, ed., *Send the Light: Lottie Moon's Letters and Other Writings* (Macon: Mercer University Press, 2002), 17.

receptive to hearing the gospel than they have been in the past?

» How can knowing that the Holy Spirit prepares unbelievers to receive the gospel encourage us to share it?

2. **Would you describe the initiative you take to evangelize as urgent or complacent?**

» What factors contribute to your sense of urgency or complacency in evangelism?

» How does your view of eternity influence your motivation to evangelize?

» How can urgent, evangelism avoid becoming intense, coercive manipulation?

3. **When you pray, do you regularly ask God to raise up and mobilize individuals to share the gospel?**

» Why or why not?

» How can praying for God to raise up personal evangelists influence your own role in sharing the gospel?

» Who are some specific people for whom you can pray that God will prompt them to begin evangelizing?

GROUP LEADER DISCUSSION GUIDE

TOPIC	ENGAGE THE GROUP	EXPLORE THE ISSUE	EXECUTE THE PLAN
1: Unbelievers' Readiness to Respond to the Gospel	• Ask the group, "Is the Holy Spirit preparing unbelievers to respond to hearing the gospel just as much today as He did during Jesus' ministry?" • Then ask, "Why or why not?"	• Ask, "Do you believe that the Spirit is at work among some people groups and/or communities around the globe, making them more receptive to hearing the gospel than they have been in the past?"	• Ask, "How can knowing that the Holy Spirit prepares unbelievers to receive the gospel encourage us to share it?"
2: Your Personal Evangelistic Initiative	• Ask the group, "Would our group's overall initiative to evangelize be characterized as urgent or complacent?"	• Ask, "What factors contribute to our sense of urgency or complacency in evangelism?" • Ask, "How should our view of eternity influence our motivation to evangelize?" • Ask, "How can urgent evangelism avoid becoming intense, coercive manipulation?"	• Ask, "What practical steps should we take to prevent ourselves from becoming complacent in our practice of evangelism?"

TOPIC	ENGAGE THE GROUP	EXPLORE THE ISSUE	EXECUTE THE PLAN
3: Prayer for Personal Evangelists to be Enlisted in the Task	• Ask the group, "When we pray, do we regularly ask God to raise up and mobilize individuals to share the gospel?" • Then ask, "Why or why not?"	• Ask, "How can praying for God to raise up personal evangelists influence our own role in sharing the gospel?"	• Ask, "How can this group encourage one another to pray more consistently for gospel workers?"

Chapter 3

Is It Biblical to Pray for the Salvation of Unbelievers?

God has honored, and in many instances has answered, the fervent prayers of believers for the salvation of unbelievers. Concerning his own salvation, L. R. Scarborough, the second president of Southwestern Baptist Theological Seminary and inaugural occupant of the first established chair of evangelism in the world ("The Chair of Fire"), recounted:

> The human beginning of the influence leading to my salvation was in the prayer of my mother in my behalf when I was an infant. She climbed out of bed, having gone down toward the grave that I might live, and crawled on her knees across the floor to my little cradle when I was three weeks of age, and prayed that God would save me in His good time and call me to preach.[1]

---

1 L. R. Scarborough, "The Evolution of a Cowboy," in L.R. Scarborough Collection, 17, Archives, A. Webb Roberts Library, Southwestern Baptist Theological Seminary, Fort Worth, Texas, n.d, 1.

In fact, research has revealed in the last two decades that regardless of their sizes or locations, Southern Baptist churches that report the highest rates of baptisms attribute praying for the salvation of unbelievers by name as an essential factor leading to their evangelistic effectiveness.[2]

Although historical examples and investigative evidence of God's blessing on believers' prayers for the salvation of the lost can be documented, do any biblical precedents exist concerning praying for the salvation of unbelievers to substantiate these examples and evidences? Yes, the Bible does, in fact, establish precedence for believers to pray for the salvation of the lost, especially considering that Jesus practiced, Paul acknowledged, and Scripture instructed prayer for the salvation of unbelievers.

The Example of Jesus

The Bible attests that Christ prayed for the lost. Concerning the suffering Servant of the Lord, Isaiah writes: "Therefore I will give [H]im the many as a portion, and [H]e will receive the mighty as spoil, because [H]e willingly submitted to death, and was counted among the rebels; yet [H]e bore the sin of many *and interceded for the rebels*" (Isa 53:12, emphasis added). In his account of the death of Jesus, Luke confirms that He interceded on behalf of those who crucified and reviled Him. He writes:

> When they arrived at the place called The Skull, they crucified [H]im there, along with the criminals, one on the right and one on the left.

---

2 Thom Rainer, *Effective Evangelistic Churches* (Nashville: Broadman & Holman, 1996), 67-71, 76-79 and Steve R. Parr, Steve Foster, David Harrill, and Tom Crites, *Georgia's Top Evangelistic Churches: Ten Lessons from the Most Effective Churches* (Duluth: Georgia Baptist Convention, 2008), 10-11, 26, 29.

Then Jesus said, "Father, forgive them, because they do not know what they are doing." And they divided [H]is clothes and cast lots.

The people stood watching, and even the leaders were scoffing: "He saved others; let [H]im save [H]imself if this is God's Messiah, the Chosen One!" The soldiers also mocked [H]im. They came offering [H]im sour wine and said, "If you are the King of the Jews, save [Y]ourself!" (Luke 23:33-36, emphasis added).

As Christ suffered for the sins of the world on the cross, He prayed for the forgiveness of the very same sinners who crucified and reviled Him. The Bible does not indicate that all, or even many, of those for whose forgiveness He prayed actually received it. Nevertheless, one of the crucified criminals who at first derided the Lord later entreated Him (Matt 27:44; Luke 23:39-43). As a result, he was forgiven of his sins and was naturalized a citizen of Paradise by the Savior who cared enough to pray for him.

The Acknowledgment of Paul

In addition, the apostle Paul acknowledged praying for the salvation of unbelieving Israel. He wrote to the believers in Rome, "Brothers and sisters, my heart's desire and *prayer to God concerning them is for their salvation*" (Rom 10:1, emphasis added). Paul's desire for the salvation of his fellow countrymen led him to pray for their salvation. Although not all Israel was saved during his lifetime, he looked forward in faith to a day when the fullness of the Gentiles' salvation would be accomplished and his prayer for Israel to be saved would be answered (Rom 11:26a).

The Instruction of Scripture

Finally, believers are commanded to pray in various ways for all people, kings, and authorities. Paul wrote,

> First of all, then, I urge that petitions, prayers, inter-cessions, and thanksgivings be made for everyone, for kings and all those who are in authority, so that we may lead a tranquil and quiet life in all godliness and dignity. This is good, and it pleases God our Sav-ior, who wants everyone to be saved and to come to the knowledge of the truth (1 Tim 2:1-4).

The apostle explained that the petitions he prescribed on behalf of "everyone, men, ... kings and all those who are in au-thority" (1) should be practiced in order to live godly and rever-ently in peace and (2) prove to be good and acceptable to God, who desires the salvation of everyone. For these reasons, the supplications, prayers, and intercessions required of believers should include a petition for the salvation of all people.

Consider that most, if not all, of the kings and authorities to whom Paul referred not only were nonbelievers, but also they had actively oppressed believers. No wonder Paul appealed to the hope of a day when believers could lead godly and reverent lives in peace, free from the threat of persecution. Such a day might have been possible if the believers in Paul's day had prayed for the salvation of these tyrannical rulers, and, as a result of hear-ing the gospel, they could have believed, thus bringing an end to their oppressiveness.

In addition, Paul claimed that praying for the salvation of all men is pleasing and acceptable to God. As Tommy Lea ex-plains, "The relative clause of v. 4 provides the basis for the assertion in v. 3 that prayer for all people is pleasing to God. The goal of the prayers Paul urged is that all people be saved. *Intercession for all people pleases the God who desires all to be saved.*"[3] God desires to see everyone be saved and come to the knowledge of the truth, though not all will do so.

Therefore, in order to lead godly and reverent lives in peace and to please God with their supplication, prayers, and intercession, Paul instructed believers to pray for the salvation of all people, great and small.

Conclusion

In a sermon entitled, *Mary Magdalene*, C.H. Spurgeon urged the following in regards to believers' responsibility to plead for the salvation of the lost:

> Until the gate of hell is shut upon a man, we must not cease to pray for him. And if we see him hugging the very doorposts of damnation, we must go to the mercy seat and beseech the arm of grace to pluck him from his dangerous position. While there is life there is hope, and although the soul is almost smothered with despair, we must not despair for it, but rather arouse ourselves to awaken the Almighty arm.[4]

On their own merits, historical examples like that of Scarborough and/or pragmatic evidences like those documented by

---

3 Thomas D. Lea and Hayne P. Griffin, Jr. *1, 2 Timothy, Titus*, The New American Commentary, vol. 34 (Nashville: Broadman & Holman, 1992), 89 [emphasis added].

4 C. H. Spurgeon, "Mary Magdalene," Sermon No. 792, January 26, 1868.

Rainer and Parr provide believers reasons to pray for the salvation of unbelievers. However, the example of Jesus, the acknowledgment of Paul, and the instruction of 1 Timothy 2:1-4, as presented above, reveal to believers their obligation to pray for the salvation of the lost.

When a believer prays for the soul of a lost person and he is subsequently saved, skeptics may attribute it to nothing more than mere coincidence. When churches pray for the salvation of unbelievers by name and effective evangelistic growth results, cynics might consider it pragmatism. However, perhaps the most appropriate label to designate believers who pray for the salvation of the lost would be "biblical."

PERSONAL REFLECTION GUIDE

1. **Can you recall any additional examples in Scripture, besides the ones listed in this chapter, in which either (1) believers are encouraged to pray for the salvation of lost or (2) believers actually pray for unbelievers to be saved?**
   - » If so, what are they, and where are they located?
   - » What do these examples teach us about the importance of praying for the lost?
2. **Is there at least one person for whose salvation you have been regularly praying? If not, for whom will you begin praying that God would bring to faith in Christ?**
   - » If you have already been praying for someone's salvation, have you observed any changes, big or small, in that person's life or his receptivity to the gospel?

» How might praying for someone's salvation lead you to evangelize him more intentionally?

GROUP LEADER DISCUSSION GUIDE

TOPIC	ENGAGE THE GROUP	EXPLORE THE ISSUE	EXECUTE THE PLAN
1: Biblical Examples of Praying for the Salvation of the Lost	• Ask the group, "Can you recall any additional scriptural examples, beyond those in this chapter, in which believers are encouraged to pray for the lost, or in which believers do pray for unbelievers to be saved?" • If so, ask, "What are they, and where are they located?"	• Ask, "What do these biblical examples teach us about the importance and power of praying for the salvation of unbelievers?"	• Ask, "How can we incorporate regular prayers for the salvation of the lost into our group's prayer time?"
2: Personal Prayer for the Salvation of Unbelievers	• Ask the group, "Who would be willing to share the first name (or a pseudonym) of someone for whose salvation they have been regularly praying?"	• Ask, "In what ways can prayer make us more intentional in sharing the gospel with those for whom we pray?"	• Ask, "Are there specific ways this group can support fellow members in their prayers for specific individuals' salvation?"

CHAPTER 4

SOIL-SPECULATIVE OR SOUL-DRIVEN EVANGELISM?

Accompanying your father on a fishing trip brings fond memories to mind—that is, as long as he isn't always catching more fish than you. I have the "blessing," as Dad calls it, or the "curse," as I refer to it, of having a father who always catches more fish than I. During the first weekend of almost every June, my father wastes no time demonstrating this fact when he and I go trout fishing on the Tuckasegee River in Jackson County, North Carolina.

Every year it's the same routine: I find a particular place in the river I'm convinced is teeming with fish, so I spend the entire morning there and catch very few fish, if any at all. On the other hand, Dad wastes no time at any one particular place. He casts the bait on his pole in one place no more than three or four times and continues that process until his bait locates a place in the river where fish are swarming. Each year dad knows he'll find me in the place where he saw me last. Inevitably he catches more fish than I, continually offering me the same advice: "Son, cast your bait all along the river and let it, not your hunch about one particular hole, bring in the catch." After years of "speculative" fishing, I'm convinced now to rely more on my bait than one notional spot.

Jesus likens, or refers to, evangelism as "fishing for men" (Matt 4:19; 13:47-50; Mark 1:17). Evangelism seems to be in mind also when He delivers His parable of a sower sowing seed (Matt 13:1-9, 18-23; Mark 4:1-9, 14-20; Luke 8:4-8, 11-15). These two metaphors assist Christians in evaluating their methods of evangelism, as well as their expectations of the results.

In this parable, Jesus likens the gospel, or the "word about the kingdom," to the sower's seed. Broadcast by the sower, seed falls either along the pathway, upon rocky ground, among thorns, or on good soil. Some disagreement exists among commentators about the kinds of responses these four soil types represent. However, Jesus' explanation of this parable seems to suggest that the three former types of soil indicate people's eventual failure to respond to the gospel's invitation, while the latter soil denotes those who understand and gladly receive the gospel.

When preaching Matthew 13:3-23, Steven Smith keenly remarked, "It is only when someone is exposed to the seed do they [or you] know what type of soil they are, and if we're not preaching the gospel to people, they [or you] don't have any way to judge who they are."[1] Believing that gospel seed manifests the type of response each person makes upon a particular time he hears the gospel, a personal evangelist should base the frequency of his evangelism upon his complete confidence in the "seed" of the gospel rather than personal conjecture about the "soil" of someone's anticipated response.

At some time or another, a personal evangelist will doubtless be tempted to base his decision to evangelize someone on his

---

1 Steven Smith, "The Gospel has a Future;" October 13, 2010; accessed on April 19, 2025, *https://equipthecalled.com/swbtsc-podcast/the-future-of-the-gospel*.

own impressions and/or speculation of that person's likelihood to profess or reject Christ at a given moment. He must resist this temptation for at least two reasons:

1. The "Parable of the Sower" (Matt 13:1-9, 18-23; Mark 4:1-9, 14-20; Luke 8:4-8, 11-15) does not substantiate soil-speculative evangelism. The sower-evangelist of these texts scatters the gospel seed indiscriminately and generously, not theoretically or hypothetically.

2. Yielding to the temptation of evangelizing only those who appear ready to respond is ultimately an attempt to access omniscience available only to God. One of the many ways Scripture attests to Jesus' divinity can be found in His ability to perceive the hearts and minds of others (*cf.*, Matt 9:3-4; Mark 2:6-8; Luke 5:21-22; 24:38; John 1:45-50; 2:24-25; 5:42; 6:61, 64). Only God, not a perceptive personal evangelist, possesses the omniscient and intimate knowledge of how anyone, at any time, will respond to a gospel appeal.

The "Parable of the Sower" reminds personal evangelists that sowers scatter seed; they do not inspect soils. In like manner, when "fishing for men," they must spend more time proclaiming the gospel of the kingdom than they do evaluating the likelihood of others' responses to the gospel. So instead of basing when and where you will "fish for men" upon a personal assumption of a "fishing hole" that appears to be teeming with bountiful catches, consider taking a wise father's advice: "Trust the constantly casted bait [of the gospel], not your hunch about one particular hole, to bring in the catch.

PERSONAL REFLECTION GUIDE

1. Before you evangelize, do you find yourself
    trusting more in your own perceived ability to
    predict how someone will respond to the gospel
    than in the gospel's power and the Holy Spirit's
    work?
    »   If so, why do you think this is the case?
    »   What way(s), if any, has your mindset changed
        in this regard based on what you learned in
        this chapter?
2. After reading Matthew 13:1-9, 18-23; Mark 4:1-
    9, 14-20; and Luke 8:4-8, 11-15, do you think
    Jesus is teaching that the gospel's success is de-
    termined by the technique by which the gospel
    is "sown" or the condition of the "soil" that re-
    ceives it?
    »   What verses support your view?
    »   How should this parable shape the way you
        share the gospel?
3. Read Isaiah 6:9-10 alongside the "Parable of the
    Sower" passages (cf., Matt 13:1-9, 18-23; Mark
    4:1-9, 14-20; Luke 8:4-8, 11-15). Is the parable's
    purpose (1) to prescribe how a personal evange-
    list should share the gospel in order to see souls
    saved or (2) to describe the types of responses
    unbelievers will make when they hear the gos-
    pel?
    »   What spiritual truths in these verses led you
        to your conclusion?

GROUP LEADER DISCUSSION GUIDE

TOPIC	ENGAGE THE GROUP	EXPLORE THE ISSUE	EXECUTE THE PLAN
1: Trusting in the Gospel's and the Spirit's Power Versus Your Own Personal Ability	• Ask the group, "Have you found yourself trusting more in your perceived ability to predict how someone will respond to the gospel than you do in the gospel's power and the Holy Spirit's work?"	• Ask, "Why might some believers rely more on their own assessment of an unbeliever's openness to the gospel than on the power of the gospel and the Holy Spirit to work, or already to be at work, in that person's life?"	• Have the group share some Scriptures that teach the power of the gospel and the Holy Spirit in the context of evangelism (*e.g.*, Rom 1:16; 1 Cor 1:18; 1 Thess 1:5). • Encourage group members either to memorize or to meditate on at least one of these verses over the next week.

TOPIC	ENGAGE THE GROUP	EXPLORE THE ISSUE	EXECUTE THE PLAN
2: Which Determines Success?: The Style of the Sowing or State of the Soil	• Have the group read Matthew 13:1-9, 18-23; Mark 4:1-9, 14-20; and Luke 8:4-8, 11-15. • Ask the group, "In this parable, on which factor does Jesus teach that the gospel's success depends: (1) the way the sower scattered the seed or (2) the pre-condition of the different kinds of soil?"	• Ask, "How should this parable shape the way believers share the gospel?"	• Have the group pray that God (1) prepares the "soil" of the hearts of unbelievers' they will encounter in the coming week and (2) prompts them to share the gospel, trusting more in His power than their methods.

CHAPTER 5

OVERCOMING FEARS
IN EVANGELISM

One evening several years ago, a Maryville, Tennessee college student named George leaped out of bed, switched on his light, and shouted to his roommate, "I've got it! I've got it!" Awakened from his sleep, the roommate asked, "What have you got, George?"

George replied, "Everyone in the U.S. has a chance to hear the gospel—but not in Mexico. We should go there this summer and distribute gospel tracts. How about it?" Stumbling over his words, the roommate said, "Well, George, I don't know. I'd have to pray about it."

"Okay, let's pray," said George as he knelt beside his bed. A couple of minutes later, George lifted his head and asked, "So, are you ready to go now?" The roommate was reluctant to finalize a commitment to go so far, so soon. George muttered, "It takes some people so long to decide to do anything!" Years later, George Verwer, the referenced, evangelistic college student, became the founder of Operation Mobilization.

Like Verwer's roommate, many believers in Jesus Christ often allow fear to become an obstacle that prevents them from evangelizing. These fear-related obstacles come in many forms. Consider the following fear-focused obstacles to evangelism, as well as some suggested ways to overcome them.

1. Fear of the Unknown Impedes Believers' Evangelism by Emphasizing Unfamiliar Experiences

Some believers do not evangelize because they do not know what to expect if they were to share the gospel with others. Perhaps they are unsure who might be inside the houses they are to visit. Maybe they are uncertain about the reaction they will receive from those sitting nearby at the local coffee shop or from their unbelieving friends.

Regarding the fear of the unknown, every believer has a choice—either allow the unknown to remain mysterious by not evangelizing, or make known the unknown by evangelizing. A believer will never know what will or will not happen in a particular witnessing situation unless he offers others a clear and complete witness to the saving power of Jesus Christ's death, burial, and resurrection and call for a decision. Of all the possible responses others can offer to believers who share the glorious gospel of Jesus Christ, more than likely, they will either want to hear more on the matter or politely decline the conversation.

2. Fear for Safety Hinders Some Believers from Evangelizing in an Effort Toward Self-Preservation

In an environment where reports of Christians' falling under attack for preaching the gospel around the globe become more and more normative, some believers naturally fear for their own safety. This news should come as no surprise to believers who follow a Savior who was despised and rejected by men to the point of His own death. In fact, when Jesus warned His followers of the dangers they would endure for His name's sake, He did not, for the sake of their own safety, excuse them from evangelizing. Rather, He charged them that "it is necessary that the gospel be preached to all nations" (Mark 13:9-13).

Although danger is not out of the realm of possibility, most believers in America need not fear for their safety while sharing the gospel in their own communities. Of course, all believers should exercise wisdom when witnessing (e.g., not trespassing on property with clearly marked "No Trespassing" signage; not aggressively arguing with someone who disagrees with gospel premises). In fact, those who evangelize on a consistent basis generally experience few, if any, dangerous encounters when evangelizing.

3. Fear of Rejection Prevents Believers from Evangelizing by Shifting Attention from Jesus to Themselves

Generally speaking, most people want to be accepted by others. Some believers do not evangelize for fear that those with whom they share the gospel might reject them when they call for decisions.

Those who battle the fear of rejection should remind themselves of the words of Jesus when He said, "But whoever denies [M]e before others, I will also deny him before [M]y Father in heaven" (Matt 10:33). When evangelizing, believers must first convey the message that only Jesus Christ can reconcile men and women to God through His death and resurrection. Then they must call their listeners to make a commitment whereby they repent of their sins and believe in Christ alone for their salvation.

After the gospel is clearly communicated to them, any rejection on the part of the evangelized is much more serious than

45

whether or not the personal evangelist has been denied. Any rejection of a clear communication of the gospel is a denial of Jesus Christ Himself. On a related note, not every time a believer evangelizes can he be guaranteed that someone will accept Christ and the free gift of forgiveness; however, a believer can be guaranteed that no one will ever accept Christ and His free gift of forgiveness if he never evangelizes.

4. Fear of Failure Obstructs Believers' Sharing the Gospel by Causing Them to Adopt a Faulty Understanding of Success

Many believers accept the false premise that evangelism is successful only if an unbeliever makes a profession of faith in Jesus Christ for his salvation. This misunderstanding, if adopted by believers, can prove devastating.

While no one will deny that a profession of faith brings great joy, encouragement, and affirmation to a personal evangelist, these results must never be equated with success. If the decisions of those who are evangelized rest solely on the abilities of believers, then perhaps believers' evangelism could be categorized in terms of success or failure; however, the decisions of those who are evangelized rest with them and the work of the Holy Spirit. Believers' success and failure in terms of evangelism is measured by their obedience or disobedience to the Great Commission of Jesus Christ.

5. Dread from Past Negative Evangelistic Experiences Promotes a Fear that Paralyzes Some Believers in Their Evangelism

Some believers do not evangelize because they fear a repeating of previous negative evangelism experiences. Whether due to their own mistakes, such as forgetting a Scripture reference or the reactions of their hearers, these negative experiences can easily sideline formerly eager witnesses. Even the memories of negative circumstances, such as seeing no one come to the door when visiting homes in a community, can elicit fear at the next opportunity for evangelism. Although many believers tend to let these negative experiences push them into evangelistic paralysis, they should instead evaluate and learn from the experiences in order to emerge stronger and ready for the next encounter.

6. Fear of Emulating Perceived Manipulation in Others' Evangelism Fosters a Desire to Overcorrect by Not Evangelizing at All

While some believers let their own negative experiences paralyze them, others focus on the perceived manipulation of others to excuse themselves from evangelizing. They cite examples of manipulative attempts at evangelism, and they overcorrect by not evangelizing at all. In reality, however, manipulation is a matter of the heart much more than it is a matter of practice. By guarding their own hearts, these believers can minimize their risk of manipulating others, who desperately need to hear the gospel proclaimed to them personally.

7. Fear of Perceived Fanaticism Promotes within Believers an Aversion to Evangelize

Other potential personal evangelists fail to share the gospel because they do not want hearers to call them "fanatics." In truth, obedient believers almost always face ridicule for evangelistically acting upon their love for Christ. They should remember that such ridicule generally stems from either misunderstanding, jealousy, or guilt. With their eyes on Christ, they must echo the apostles' determination to obey God rather than men (Acts 5:29).

Their concern about the opinions of others will fade in the light of Christ's approval.

8. An Absence of the Fear of God Strips Believers of a Healthy Motivation to Evangelize the Lost

To this point in the discussion, believers have been encouraged to shun fears that become obstacles to evangelism. However, all believers must embrace the fear of God in order to motivate their witness for Christ.

The apostle Paul wrote, "Therefore, since we know the fear of the Lord, we try to persuade people. ... Therefore, we are ambassadors for Christ, since God is making [H]is appeal through us. We plead on Christ's behalf: 'Be reconciled to God'" (2 Cor 5:11, 20). In his commentary on 2 Corinthians in the *New American Commentary* series, David Garland explains that fear, in this textual context, refers to "a religious consciousness, a reverential awe of God, that directs the way one lives."[1] Believers who consistently live devoid of the fear of God will, at best, forfeit heavenly rewards and, at worst, feel apathy towards the salvation of the lost.

Aware of the day he would appear before the *bema* seat of Christ (2 Cor 5:10), Paul sought to persuade, implore, and plead with others to be reconciled to God by proclaiming the gospel of Jesus Christ. Believers must fear God because they, like Paul, will one day stand before the *bema* seat of our Lord and give account for what they have and have not done during their lives, including the extent of their faithfulness in evangelism. Christ's judgment at the *bema* seat will result either in receiving or in forfeiting heavenly, eternal rewards.

Much more urgent than what heavenly rewards believers will or will not receive, the fear of God reminds personal evan-

---

1 David Garland, *2 Corinthians*, New American Commentary (Nashville: B&H, 1999), 269-270.

gelists of His impending wrath and judgment upon unbelievers. While believers will appear before the *bema* seat of Christ, all unbelievers will appear before the Great White Throne to be judged and condemned (Rev 20:11-15). Those who appear at this judgment will be punished eternally in the lake of fire because they have neglected to respond in repentance and faith in Jesus Christ. Believers must embrace the fear of God that leads them to evangelize in order that they might avoid adopting an uncompassionate apathy for the final state of the lost.

Doubtless, all believers at some time or another face one or more of these fear-related obstacles to evangelism. The two primary and greatest catalysts for overcoming fear-related obstacles to one's personal practice of evangelism include (1) the convicting power of the Word of God and (2) the empowering ability of the Holy Spirit. As you read the Bible for conviction and pray for divine empowerment in order to conquer fear-based obstacles in evangelism, consider identifying which of the fear-related obstacles threaten your evangelistic faithfulness, and then apply the particular suggestions offered above that address them.

George Verwer was known to encourage others to evangelize with the impassioned plea, "We are God's chosen people, not his frozen people, so let's pray for defrost!" May fear-related obstacles no longer freeze beautiful feet in their tracks from proclaiming the good news of Jesus Christ for salvation.

PERSONAL REFLECTION GUIDE

1. **What fear(s) make it hardest for you to share the gospel?**
    » Are there any practical strategies or mindsets, besides those mentioned in this chapter,

49

that can help you or other believers overcome those fears? If so, what are they?

2. **How does God-centered fear, as discussed in the eighth principle of this chapter, differ from all the other man-centered fears that are described in principles one through seven?**

   » How can you intentionally grow in a healthy fear of the Lord to replace fear of people in order to motivate you to evangelize?

GROUP LEADER DISCUSSION GUIDE

TOPIC	ENGAGE THE GROUP	EXPLORE THE ISSUE	EXECUTE THE PLAN
1: Identifying Fears that Hinder Evangelism	• Ask the group, "What fears do you find most challenging when it comes to sharing the gospel?"	• Ask, "Who can suggest some practical strategies or mindsets, beyond those offered in the chapter, that will help believers overcome these fears?"	• Have group members share specific fears that hinder them from sharing the gospel. • Divide the group into small teams, and instruct them to pray for the Holy Spirit to help their team members overcome any evangelistic fears they have.

TOPIC	ENGAGE THE GROUP	EXPLORE THE ISSUE	EXECUTE THE PLAN
2: Growing in God-Centered Fear	• Ask the group, "How does the fear of God, as described in the chapter's eighth principle, differ from all the other man-centered fears that were discussed?"	• Ask, "How does the fear of the Lord affect our approach to sharing the gospel differently than the fear of people does?"	• Have the group read Deuteronomy 10:12; Proverbs 1:7; 9:10; Psalm 34:7; 110:10; Ecclesiastes 12:13; and/or 2 Corinthians 5:11. • Ask, "How can these verses encourage boldness in evangelism?" • Encourage group members either to memorize or to meditate on at least one of these verses over the next week.

CHAPTER 6

FINDING EVANGELISTIC CONFIDENCE

Instead of seeking after the lost, many believers spend time searching for the confidence to evangelize. They tell themselves, "If only I had more confidence, I would share the gospel with my friends and acquaintances that I know need Christ." Imagine how much confidence they believe they might need to share Christ with someone who is hostile to the gospel.

In the middle of the last century, a rodeo clown and steer wrestler named Ken Boen lived in Fort Smith, Arkansas. Boen was hostile to the gospel and had a reputation in the area as the last person in the world who would ever receive Christ. A number of pastors, evangelists, and lay people attempted to share the gospel with him, and he invariably rejected their offers to receive Christ. In fact, almost no believer in Fort Smith had any confidence when it came to evangelizing Boen because of the hardness of his heart.

Have you ever been in need of evangelistic confidence? Every believer, at some time or another, has needed evangelistic confidence. One way that personal evangelists have found confidence over the years has been to enroll in evangelism training. Evangelism training has provided willing personal evangelists confidence by teaching them a gospel script that they can memorize so they would know what to say when they evangelize.

While evangelism training can provide willing personal evangelists with confidence to know what to say, it does not necessarily always give them confidence to begin evangelistic conversations. How, then, do personal evangelists find the confidence to share the gospel with those who are open to hear it as well as with those who are hostile against it? Consider the evangelistic confidence of Peter and John as recorded in Acts 4:13-20. Having healed a lame man in the name of Jesus (3:1-10), Peter and John preach the resurrection from the dead through Jesus in Jerusalem (3:11-26; 4:1-2). The priests, the captain of the temple guard, and the Sadducees take offense and arrest them (4:1-3). Nevertheless, 5,000 of those hearing their message believe in Jesus (4:4).

The next day, the apostles are put on trial. Their accusers ask, "By what power, or in what name, have you done this" (4:5-7)? With complete confidence and filled with the Holy Spirit, Peter replies that they did this in the name of Jesus Christ the Nazarene (4:8-12). Then, Acts 4:13-20 records:

> When they *observed the boldness* of Peter and John and *realized that they were uneducated and untrained men, they were amazed and recognized that they had been with Jesus.* And since they saw the man who had been healed standing with them, they had nothing to say in opposition.
>
> After they ordered them to leave the Sanhedrin, they conferred among themselves, saying, "What should

we do with these men? For an obvious sign has been done through them, clear to everyone living in Jerusalem, and we cannot deny it. But so that it does not spread any further among the people, let's threaten them against speaking to anyone in this name again."

So they called for them and ordered them not to speak or teach at all in the name of Jesus. *Peter and John answered them, "Whether it's right in the sight of God for us to listen to you rather than to God, you decide; for we are unable to stop speaking about what we have seen and heard"* (emphasis added).

Notice that the members of the Sanhedrin in amazement observe Peter and John's confidence in spite of the fact that they are both uneducated and untrained men. They attribute the apostles' confidence to the fact that they have been with Jesus.

If believers know enough of the gospel to have been saved by it, then they know enough of the gospel to share it with others. Evangelistic confidence is not attained merely by what believers know (such as a memorized, evangelistic script); it is attained by Whom they know—that is, Jesus Christ.

Many believers today have received more evangelism training than those in the early church did. How, then, did early believers know what to say when they evangelized? What was the secret of their evangelistic confidence? They had been with Jesus (4:13). They remembered what they had seen (4:20). They recalled what they had heard (4:20). Those seeking evangelistic confidence will find it whenever they spend time with Jesus. Those who spend time with Jesus cannot help but spend time telling others about Jesus. Furthermore, those with whom we spend time telling about Jesus can tell whether or not we have spent time with Jesus (4:13).

In 1953 well-known evangelist J. Harold Smith was called to serve as the pastor of the First Baptist Church of Fort Smith, Arkansas. As a man who walked with God, Smith, like Peter and John, confidently told almost everyone with whom he came into contact about Jesus Christ. Not long after assuming his new pastorate, Smith heard about Ken Boen. Despite Boen's reputation of having a hardened heart to the gospel, Smith paid him a visit at his home. He was not confident that Boen would receive Christ, but he was confident that Jesus would be with him when he went.

Dressed in his best Sunday suit and shoes, Smith gingerly stepped around and over mud puddles to meet Boen, who was in the field tending to his horses. Boen listened to the pastor-evangelist as he shared the gospel with him. Smith then asked him if he would be willing to receive Jesus Christ as His Lord and Savior. Boen's eyes scanned the preacher from his head to his toes, looked at the mud puddles all around his feet, and then peered deeply into Smith's eyes. He replied, "Preacher, if you are willing to bend down on your knees with me to pray right now, then I am willing to receive Christ right now." With no hesitation at all, Smith confidently bent down in the mud. Though the evangelist's clean suit and shoes became a muddy mess, the steer wrestler's filthy heart was made clean as he, too, bent to his knees and received Jesus Christ as his Lord and Savior.

May we consistently spend time with Jesus so that we might display similar boldness and confidence in sharing His gospel.

PERSONAL REFLECTION GUIDE

1. **Does a lack of confidence keep you from sharing the gospel?**
   » If so, is it because you are unsure what to say?
   » Think about the person who shared the gospel with you. What part of their message led you to repent of your sins and believe in Jesus?
   » What were the essential truths they shared (*e.g.*, sin; Christ's death/burial/resurrection; a call to repent and believe)? How can remembering that simple message help you confidently share it with others?

2. **Do you consistently spend time with Jesus by daily reading Scripture and praying?**
   » If so, do people around you recognize that you have "been with Jesus," as the Sanhedrin did of Peter and John (*cf.*, Acts 4:13)?
   » If not, what adjustments could you make to your quiet time in an effort to motivate your desire to tell others about Christ?

GROUP LEADER DISCUSSION GUIDE

TOPIC	ENGAGE THE GROUP	EXPLORE THE ISSUE	EXECUTE THE PLAN
1: Confidence in Evangelism	• Ask the group, "How many of you lack confidence in sharing the gospel?" • Ask, "Why do we sometimes struggle to feel confident in sharing the gospel with others (e.g., not knowing what to say; not knowing how the other person will respond)?"	• Invite members of the group to share a brief summary of the gospel message they remember from the person who shared it with them. • Next, confirm with the group whether or not the message of the gospel they recalled includes everything an unbeliever needs to hear in order to repent and believe. (If it does not, then discuss and identify what else should be included. If it does, then encourage them with this truth: "If you know enough of the gospel to be saved by it, then you know enough of the gospel to share it.")	• Review and summarize the essential gospel truths (e.g., sin; Christ's death/burial/ resurrection; a call to repent and believe) in order to help build the group's confidence to evangelize.

TOPIC	ENGAGE THE GROUP	EXPLORE THE ISSUE	EXECUTE THE PLAN
2: Consistent Time with Jesus	• Ask the group to share the challenges they face in maintaining a consistent quiet time. • Ask them how their personal relationship with Jesus affects their confidence in sharing the gospel.	• Invite the group to suggest ways that their quiet times might be enriched in order to inspire and motivate them to share the gospel with greater frequency and urgency.	• Challenge group members to commit to a set number of quiet time days over the next week and to come prepared to share their experiences of how it inspired them to share Christ at the next meeting.

CHAPTER 7

COMMON APPROACHES TO SHARE THE GOSPEL

M any Christians have never adopted any specific approach to share Christ regularly. Those who have; however, usually prefer one evangelism method over all others. For a host of reasons, ranging from sincerely-held beliefs to narrow-mindedness, the value that some personal evangelists place on their own personal evangelism technique leads them to criticize all other approaches, as well as those who have adopted them.

So, what is the best evangelism method for believers to use? The worst method is the one they know but never use. The best approach is the one they actually practice. As Roy Fish is reported to have said to his "Introduction to Evangelism" students, "The only approach worse than a bad approach is no approach at all."

This chapter analyzes six common approaches to sharing the gospel and includes some additional evangelism tips. Each of these approaches has potential strengths and weaknesses, but not all approaches are created equal. They all have their own advantages and usefulness in particular situations; therefore, effective personal evangelists should learn how to utilize more than one of these approaches while guarding against adopting their potentially noted weaknesses. The leading of the Holy Spirit should dictate which approach, or approaches, should be incorporated in any given evangelistic encounter.

The Witness

The *Witness* uses his testimony to present the gospel. A narrative approach is ideal when a believer is sitting next to someone else on a plane. For example, the believer can make small talk and ask the other person what he does for a living. Typically, as the conversation progresses, the person will ask the Christian about himself. At this point, he should share with the other person a little about his own life, and then bridge the conversation into an opportunity to share a testimony of how Christ saved him.

Sharing a testimony is a strong approach because it is natural and relational. However, one weakness to this approach is that a believer who utilizes his can sometimes get bogged down in sharing his story such that the conversation either gets sidetracked or never contains an explicit explanation of the gospel.

In order to overcome this outcome, a believer should have a three-part, mental outline prepared: (1) what life was like before Christ; (2) how he came to Christ; and (3) what his life has been like since coming to Christ. He should be careful not to spend the majority of the time on his life before Christ or after Christ. Instead, he should spend the most time on how he came to Christ, which should be a re-telling of the good news that will enable him to include an explicit gospel presentation.

The Inquisitor

The *Inquisitor* asks questions that lead the conversation to a point at which he can directly share the gospel. Jesus serves as the best model of this questioning approach, as demonstrated in His conversation with the woman at the well (*cf.*, John 4:1-26). Randy Newman's book, *Questioning Evangelism*, is an excellent resource for those interested in learning more about this approach.

One potential weakness of this approach is that the other person may feel defensive if the believer bombards him with too many questions. Additionally, when a personal evangelist asks an extroverted stranger a series of questions, the stranger might dominate the conversation with his answers, leaving the believer no time to share the gospel.

To avoid these dangers, a believer should stick to a brief set of questions that are direct and intentional. He should avoid general, open-ended questions. He will want to have in mind a blueprint in which he can drive conversations directly to the death of Christ and His resurrection from the dead.

The Analogist

The *Analogist* utilizes his environment, circumstances, situations, and current events to lead a conversation to the gospel. Examples of this approach include talking to his doctor about the Great Physician or connecting a news story to the evil and hopelessness in our world.

Of course, one liability to this approach is that it may sound like a good connection in the personal evangelist's mind but sound tacky to everyone else. Another hazard is that an argument could ensue about opposing political or economic views and derail an opportunity to get to the gospel. However, the strength in this approach is that it is natural, conversational, and effective in bridging dialogues to the gospel.

The Server

The *Server* serves others through either planned or spontaneous acts of service in order to create an opportunity to evangelize another. Examples include servanthood evangelism, mercy ministries, and random acts of kindness. This approach demonstrates compassion and concern on behalf of the personal evangelist for the other person(s).

While personal evangelists must demonstrate genuine concern for unbelievers, this approach has the potential to lead them to adopt some unwise evangelism philosophies and practices. For example, some *Servers* will convince themselves that they must earn a right to evangelize a stranger. Attempting to earn a right to evangelize can foster a *quid pro quo* kind of evangelism, in which personal evangelists foster an expectation that those who receive their acts of service must listen to their gospel presentations or feel guilty for not doing so. *Servers* who adopt this philosophy and practice should remind themselves that as Lord, Jesus has "earned" the right to command us to adopt the biblical philosophy and practice of evangelizing as many as possible, as soon as possible.

Over time, other well-meaning *Servers* will be tempted to follow the path of social gospel advocates by confusing benevolence with evangelism or by promoting an unhealthy interdependence between gospel proclamation and mercy ministry. Believers have an obligation to practice both gospel proclamation and mercy ministry without the self-imposed guilt or expectation that they must do one in order to do the other.

Jesus, who healed many infirmities and provided food for the multitudes' hunger, stated that He came "to seek and save the lost" (Luke 19:10). If evangelism is relegated to nothing more than the practice of social services to those in need, then it follows that many people, including atheists, Muslims, Hindus, and Buddhists, evangelize. If this is the case (and it is not!), then it follows that by way of their compassionate actions they, like personal evangelists who simultaneously share the gospel and serve the needs of others, practice Christian evangelism. Everyday personal evangelists should practice compassion and even meet physical needs, when possible, as they evangelize; but they should prioritize the practice of biblical evangelism, as they alone can offer the Bread of Life (John 6:31-35, 48, 50-51, 58).

Last, *Servers* should be prepared to practice other evangelistic approaches, as well. If they are not, they will find that they can evangelize only those who have needs the personal evangelists themselves can meet. Those utilizing the *Server* approach and no other approach(es) must be reminded that Jesus died to save those who have no discernible physical needs (*e.g.*, the rich), as well as those who have needs greater than *Servers* can meet. *Servers* have a responsibility to proclaim the gospel to these groups, too!

The Networker

In his desire to be incarnational, the *Networker* meets and befriends others with the intent to evangelize them. The relational nature between the personal evangelist and the other person (1) allows for further discussion of questions about the gospel; (2) demonstrates for the other person a Christian lifestyle; and (3) fosters a relationship that will prove helpful for subsequent discipleship if the other person professes faith in Christ.

Networkers will be tempted to delay evangelizing their newfound friends for fear of a negative effect on the relationships they seek to establish. Tommy Kiker tells the story of a missionary who left America to live in another country. Almost immediately, he made friends with one of the citizens; however, he assumed that his new friend was not ready to hear the gospel. After several months, the missionary was reassigned and scheduled a meeting with this friend to say goodbye. The missionary looked deeply into the eyes of his friend and said, "I have bad news. The company for which I work has relocated me, so I will have to leave. Over the last several months, I have grown to love you as a dear friend, so before I leave, I want to share with you the most important thing I could ever share with you." The friend stopped the missionary and said, "If what you have to share is so important, then why did you not share it with me earlier?"

Personal evangelists in the New Testament did not make friends with strangers in order to become acclimated with them over an extended period of time and then tell them about Christ. Rather, they shared Christ with strangers and, as a result, relationships, sometimes in the context of a local church, were established.

Also, *Networkers* should be careful in their attempts to prepare new acquaintances to hear the gospel after they have established a "sufficient" amount of trust (in whatever way(s) that could be measured). Such an attempt can lead would-be personal evangelists to emphasize relationship building to the neglect of acknowledging (1) the Holy Spirit's preparing unbelievers' hearts to receive the gospel and (2) the uncertain guarantee that they will have future opportunities to share the gospel. For example, how can personal evangelists know to what extent the Holy Spirit has prepared others' hearts to receive the message of the gospel if they have not shared the gospel with them (*cf.*, Matt 13:1-9, 18-23)? Personal evangelists can never know how another person will respond to the gospel until they have first shared the gospel with him. Other questions to consider include the following: (1) What certainty do personal evangelists have that they will be able to meet with their new acquaintances/friends long enough to build a "sufficient" level of trust in order to share the gospel with them? (2) What if their new acquaintances/friends do not want to meet again? (3) What if they die before "sufficient" trust is built? and (4) What if Jesus returns before they ever hear the gospel?

The Charging Bull

The *Charging Bull* comes out of nowhere, rushes in on an unsuspecting stranger, and launches into an evangelistic presentation before the other person even knows the name of the aggressive personal evangelist. Like a bull in a china shop, he does not seek to build bridges in the conversation or to develop a relationship. He forcibly takes control of the conversation in such a way that he almost takes his listener captive.

While this person can be applauded for being very direct and intentional in evangelism, this approach often forces the conversation and can lend itself to manipulation or the other person's feeling pressured. When this happens, the listener will either change the subject or, worse, oblige to make a "profession of faith" out of fear or under duress just to get the *Charing Bull* to "stampede" elsewhere. The *Bull* also has a tendency to focus on his ability to convince an unbeliever to do what the personal evangelist wants him to do rather than the Holy Spirit to convict the unbeliever of his need for Christ.

Personal evangelism occurs in the context of conversations, not monologues. Those practicing personal evangelism as though it is a one-sided conversation will see their listeners tune out for lack of interest. Everyday personal evangelists should present as much of the gospel as possible to their listeners, while also encouraging feedback so that their gospel presentations can naturally address listeners' specific situations rather than sounding canned and forced.

Some Advice for Improving Your Personal Evangelism

After identifying your natural approaches to evangelism and safeguarding yourself against their potential pitfalls and weaknesses, use the following tips to assist you as you practice everyday evangelism:

» **Be intentional about starting conversations with people in public.** Get into the habit of speaking to strangers and making small talk.

» **If you struggle with motivation or fear, ask yourself this question:** "Am I willing to take the chance that someone else either has in the past or will in the future share the gospel with this person?" You cannot know the extent to which he has heard the gospel during past conversations or will hear it in future ones, but you can be sure that he will hear the gospel during the course of your conversation if you actually share it with him.

» **Always carry a gospel tract.** If the person seems disinterested, the conversation gets interrupted, or you share the gospel and he rejects it, you can always leave a tract with him to read at a later time.

» **Always call for a response to the gospel.** No gospel presentation is complete without inviting the person to repent of his sins and place his faith in Christ.

» **Always offer to pray for the person.** Prayer often opens doors to an evangelistic conversation, even with someone who might otherwise seem disinterested.

PERSONAL REFLECTION GUIDE

1. **Do you have a particular approach you use when you evangelize?**
   » If so, is it one of the approaches presented in this chapter or a different one?
   » If not, is there an approach from this chapter you would like to learn?
2. **If you utilize one of the approaches in this chapter, have you noticed you have also adopted one or more its weaknesses?**
   » If so, which weakness(es)?
   » How do you intend to correct the problem(s)?
3. **After reading the chapter, do you see any benefit in learning more than only one approach to evangelize?**
   » If so, which method would you like to learn next?

GROUP LEADER DISCUSSION GUIDE

TOPIC	ENGAGE THE GROUP	EXPLORE THE ISSUE	EXECUTE THE PLAN
1: Identifying a Personal Approach to Evangelism	• Invite group members to share their preferred evangelism approaches.	• Invite group members to present the reasons they prefer their particular evangelistic approaches.	• Have group members list the strengths of their preferred approaches and explain how they help them share the gospel.

TOPIC	ENGAGE THE GROUP	EXPLORE THE ISSUE	EXECUTE THE PLAN
2: Recognizing Weaknesses in Our Approach	• Invite the group to share examples of challenges or limitations they have noticed when using their personal approaches to evangelism.	• Lead the group to identify and discuss biblical correctives to these weaknesses.	• Have the group create a short list of practical steps, based on biblical principles, they can take to address these weaknesses in the coming week.
3: The Value of Learning Multiple Approaches	• Ask the group, "What could be the benefits of having more than one approach to evangelism?"	• Discuss situations in which one method might be more effective than another, using real-life or hypothetical scenarios.	• Ask each group member to select a method with which they are less familiar, and pray over the coming week for an opportunity to practice it. Encourage the group to come prepared to share their experiences at the next meeting.

CHAPTER 8

QUESTIONING YOUR EVANGELISM

A lady once criticized the evangelism methods used by Dwight L. Moody, famed 19th-century American pastor, to win people to saving faith in the Lord Jesus Christ. In response, Moody replied, "I agree with you. I don't like the way I do it either. Tell me, how do you do it?" Moody's critic answered, "I don't do it." Moody quipped, "In that case, I like my way of doing it better than your way of not doing it."

Like Moody, I would rather be a criticized personal evangelist than a non-evangelistic critic. Sometimes another's critique of our evangelism is biblically warranted. At other times critical comments about our evangelism discourage us without cause. Perhaps the evangelistic enterprise would be served best if before (1) we critique and/or question the evangelistic practices of someone else and/or (2) our evangelistic practices are critiqued and/or questioned by someone else, we sternly look ourselves in the mirror and say, "I question your evangelism!"

What questions might a believer ask himself in order to assess his evangelistic practices? In *Tell It Often–Tell It Well*, Mark McCloskey suggests three essential questions every believer should ask himself in order to assess his evangelistic practices and methods biblically. In addition to McCloskey's three questions (included and enumerated in the following list of questions), I suggest five additional questions. A believer's response to each of these eight questions will assist him in discerning whether or not someone else's critique of his evangelism proves warranted, and/or what aspects of his evangelism fall short of the biblical ideal and need adjusting.

1. Is My Evangelism Consistent with the Teachings of the New Testament?[1]

Evangelism finds its origin in the New Testament. A believer who assesses his evangelistic practices should begin by ensuring his evangelism conforms to the evangelistic doctrines, instructions, and principles found in the New Testament. McCloskey offers a couple of follow-up questions that frame the context of this particular question for personal evangelistic assessment. These questions include the following: "Is my approach to evangelism grounded in theological convictions regarding salvation, the gospel, and evangelism? Is it grounded in the certainties of God's plan to redeem a lost creation, the lostness of man, and the responsibilities of our ambassadorship?"[2]

Even the most passionate person about evangelism can either (1) hold to erroneous theological convictions or (2) alter his theological convictions over time. A believer's theological convictions concerning salvation inevitably contribute to the gospel content he presents to unbelievers. Therefore, a personal evange-

---

1 Mark McCloskey, *Tell it Often-Tell it Well: Making the Most of Witnessing Opportunities* (San Bernardino: Here's Life, 1986. Reprint, Nashville: Thomas Nelson, 1995), 185.

2 McCloskey, *Tell it Often-Tell it Well*, 185.

list's theological convictions and the message he proclaims must be tested continually by New Testament doctrine, instructions, and principles. Because it serves as the authoritative and foundational source for evangelism, the New Testament must inform the reasons for and the ways in which a believer evangelizes.

2. Does My Evangelism Resemble the Way the First-Century Church Evangelized?[3]

The first-century church initially received the Great Commission of our Lord, who passed it down to all ages of His church. For this reason, a believer interested in assessing his evangelism should consider the philosophy, practice, and pattern of the apostolic church. To assist someone in this dimension of his evangelistic assessment, McCloskey suggests the following supplemental considerations: "Has my philosophy and practice of evangelism been modeled by the first-century church? Have the theological realities that drove the first-century church to proclaim the gospel with boldness and sensitivity caused me to develop similar patterns for communicating my faith?"[4] The extent to which someone's evangelism is considered biblical can be accurately measured only by his evangelistic consistency with the philosophy, practice, and pattern of the early church.

The first-century church employed an evangelistic philosophy that endeavored to evangelize as many as possible, as quickly as possible, and as clearly as possible. Though they employed other evangelistic methods, Luke recorded numerous times in which the apostles (*e.g.*, Acts 2:12-41; 3:11-26; 4:5-12; 5:19-21), deacons (*e.g.*, Acts 6:8-7:60; 8:4-6, 12, 40), and disciples (*e.g.*, Acts 2:5-11) of the early church evangelized as many peo-

3 McCloskey, *Tell it Often-Tell it Well*, 185-186.
4 McCloskey, *Tell it Often-Tell it Well*, 185-186.

ple as possible by preaching the gospel publicly. The New Testament does not include instances in which Christians evangelized unbelievers through a long-term process of building friendships and sharing minute snippets of the gospel with the same person *over* an extended period of time. Rather, it shows that they evangelized unbelievers by sharing complete presentations of the gospel *at* specific points in time (*e.g.*, John 3:1-12; 4:1-42; Acts 16:6-15; 17:16-34; 24:1-27).

Additionally, members of the first-century church also evangelized as quickly as possible. The New Testament indicates at least two reasons for the rapid rate of their evangelistic endeavors—enthusiasm and obedience. First, in order that the gospel of Jesus Christ not "*spread* any further among the people," the elders, rulers, and scribes charged Peter and John not to speak or teach in the name of Jesus (Acts 4:17-20, emphasis added). However, Peter and John enthusiastically claimed that they could not help but speak of what they had seen and heard. Second, upon being brought back before the Jewish council a second time for evangelizing in the temple, the high priest questioned why Peter and John continued to "*fill* Jerusalem" with their teaching (Acts 5:27-29, emphasis added). Peter and John responded that they must obey God and not men.

In addition to their evangelistic philosophy and practice, the first-century believers also modeled life patterns that should accompany a personal evangelist's gospel proclamation. He will face temptations to adopt worldly, even sinful, standards in order to gain a hearing and become relevant.[5] Nevertheless, he must

---

5 Though not commenting on this particular temptation, Edward Rommen articulates the danger of yielding to such a temptation when he writes: "We are under great pressure to adapt the [g]ospel to its cultural surroundings. While there is a legitimate concern for contextualization, what most often happens in these cases is an outright capit-

be convinced that his evangelistic proclamation should coincide with his exhibiting a pattern, or lifestyle, of biblical holiness. While not every evangelistic approach practiced today can be found in the Scriptures (*i.e.*, online evangelism), an evangelistic practice consistent with them conforms to their standards of holiness, as the first-century church both believed and modeled.

3. Does My Obedience to Evangelize Conform to Jesus' Authoritative Command in the Great Commission?

McCloskey suggests we ought not to ask ourselves, "'Why are men not coming to us?' Rather we must ask ourselves, 'Why are we not going to men?'"[6] Though many symptoms prevent us from going to men with the gospel, they all result from disobedience to Jesus' authoritative command in the Great Commission.

In his day, William Carey confronted such disobedience when he published *An Enquiry into the Obligations of Christians to Use Means for the Conversion of the Heathens*. He described the Great Commission disobedience of believers in his day when he wrote:

> [B]ut the work has not been taken up, or prosecuted of late years (except by a few individuals) with the zeal and perseverance with which the primitive Christians went about it. It seems as if many thought the commission was sufficiently put in execution by what the apostles and others have done; that we have

---

ulation of the [g]ospel to the principles of that culture." *Get Real: On Evangelism in the Late Modern World* (Pasadena: William Carey Library, 2010), 371.

6 McCloskey, *Tell it Often-Tell it Well*, 191.

enough to do to attend to the salvation of our own countrymen; and that, if God intends the salvation of the heathen, he will some way or the other bring them to the gospel, or the gospel to them. It is thus that multitudes sit at ease and give themselves no concern about the far greater part of their fellow-sinners, who to this day, are lost in ignorance and idolatry. There seems also to be an opinion existing in the minds of some, that because the apostles were extraordinary officers and have no proper successors, and because many things which were right for them to do would be utterly unwarrantable for us, therefore it may not be immediately binding on us to execute the commission, though it was so upon them.[7]

Nevertheless, Carey contended that all believers have a duty to obey the Great Commission of our Lord. Otherwise, he argued, why do we continue to baptize in obedience to His command? Why do we honor the obedience of others who have evangelized throughout history? Why, then, do we believe we have available to us the divine promise of His Presence?[8]

Evangelism is not the result of mere coincidence. Evangelism rarely occurs when someone relegates it to a pastime activity. Those who fail to plan time to practice obedient evangelism will fail to find time to be obedient in evangelism. Evangelism ensues when a believer in Jesus Christ submits himself to the authoritative command of Jesus by regularly attempting to make baptized and obedient disciples.

---

7 William Carey, *An Enquiry into the Obligations of Christians to Use Means for the Conversion of the Heathens* (Leicester: n.p., 1792), 8.

8 Consult Carey, *An Enquiry into the Obligations of Christians*, 8-9.

4. Does My Evangelism Exhibit a Kind of Urgency that Takes into Account the Reality of Heaven and Hell?

Concerning the reality of heaven and hell, evangelism can be described in terms of opposite extremes—either lethargic or urgent. Though most evangelicals identify themselves as believing exclusivists, those who exercise a less-than-urgent kind of evangelism appear as practicing universalists.[9] If heaven and hell really exist and someone's eternal destiny in one or the other depends on whether or not he repents of his sins and believes in Jesus Christ's death, burial, and resurrection for salvation; how then will he hear, in order to believe and be saved, if he does not receive the gospel through evangelistic means (*cf.*, Rom 10:14-17)?

Some well-meaning pundits and commentators have critiqued urgent evangelism driven by the reality of heaven and hell. Their critiques do not dispute the reality of hell; rather, they indicate that urgent evangelism motivated by final states minimizes the importance of discipleship or that it attempts to influence hearers to profess Christ out of a fear of hell. Although the practices of a few modern-day personal evangelists may validate these concerns on occasion, urgent evangelism in light of the reality of heaven and hell (as one observes was practiced in the New Testament and as faithful, Great Commission believers practice today) neither precludes discipleship nor necessitates the use of fear tactics. As long as personal evangelists ground

---

9 In fact, Mark Terry says, "Professor Roy Fish of Southwestern Baptist Seminary has stated that most Christians are functional universalists. A universalist believes that all people will ultimately be saved. Most believers reject that concept, but they live as if they believe it because they never witness to others." *Church Evangelism: Basic Principles, Diverse Models* (Nashville: Broadman & Holman, 1997), 11.

their evangelism in the authoritative command of Jesus in the Great Commission, they will evangelize in such a way that anticipates the disciples they make through evangelism will profess their faith through believer's baptism and be taught obedience to all the commands of Christ (Matt 28:19-20).

In addition, any evangelistic discussion about hell will illicit fear in the hearts of those who listen—and it should; however, as long as the motives of personal evangelists arise from a sincere concern to convey the entire counsel of God in their evangelism rather than to manipulate, such a fear in the hearts of their hearers is a healthy one.

5. Do I Consider the Holy Spirit's Role in My Evangelism?

According to the Bible, a personal evangelist and the Holy Spirit cooperatively partner with one another in the evangelistic enterprise (Isa 53:1; Rev 22:17). Evangelism that fails to depend upon the Spirit of God has a tendency to become manipulative. On the other hand, the Holy Spirit does not evangelize on His own apart from the evangelistic witness of a believer. Rather, He assists a believer in his proclamation of the gospel to an unbeliever.

The New Testament teaches that the Holy Spirit precedes evangelistic conversations (Acts 10:1-15), convicts unbelievers of sin, righteousness, and judgment (John 16:8-11), and regenerates repentant sinners who believe in Christ for salvation (John 3:5-6). Taking into account the multifaceted roles of the Holy Spirit in evangelism, a personal evangelist must rely on the Holy Spirit in preceding (*e.g.*, Acts 8:27-35; 10:19-22), empowering (*e.g.*, Acts 1:8; 6:10), and emboldening (*e.g.*, Acts 4:8-13, 29-31) his witness, as well as convicting an unbeliever of his sin and need for Christ (*e.g.,* John 16:8-11) and sealing him for salvation after he hears the gospel and believes in Christ (*e.g.,* Eph 1:13-14).

These days, some experts tout one particular way to package the gospel in order to evangelize successfully. Other specialists prescribe the primacy of a long-term relationship over that of a comprehensive gospel proclamation in order to evangelize missionally. Still other authorities advocate the dumbing down of holiness standards in order to evangelize persuasively. Altogether, these kinds of strategies create a new form of pragmatism—method-dependent evangelism that deemphasizes and/or neglects the role and power of the Holy Spirit in a personal evangelist who proclaims as much of the gospel to as many as possible, as quickly as possible, and as clearly as possible. A believer who evangelizes without utilizing a helpful technique may experience frustration; however, a believer who evangelizes without depending on the Holy Spirit will find failure.

6. Do I Incorporate the Scriptures into My Evangelism?

The previous assessment questions appeal to evangelism that incorporates a biblical model derived from the New Testament, the practice of the first-century church, and the Great Commission. This question, on the other hand, helps believers assess the extent to which they include the Scriptures in their gospel presentations. The New Testament presents two obvious reasons for incorporating the Scriptures in gospel presentations. First, hearing the Word of Christ is a prerequisite for biblical faith (Rom 10:17). Second, evangelistic proclamations in the New Testament overwhelmingly incorporate the Scriptures (*e.g.,* Luke 24:14-32; Acts 2:14-41; 3:11-26; 4:1-12; 7:2-53; 8:4, 35; 13:13-49; 16:25-32; 17:10-13; 18:5, 28; 20:27; 26:22-23; 28:23-27).

Sadly, several of today's would-be personal evangelists utilize general revelation (*i.e.*, creation) more than they do special revelation (*i.e.*, the Bible) in their evangelism. Other personal evangelists often summarize the gospel in their own words or in the words of someone else—that is, if they utilize a witness training model. Whether they appeal to creation or use their own (or scripted) words in presenting the gospel message, personal evangelists should ensure that their evangelistic proclamations incorporate and structure themselves around the Word of God. When they evangelize, personal evangelists must incorporate Scripture in their presentations of the gospel in such a way that proves consistent with both the text's immediate context and intended meaning. Only through hearing the Scriptures can those whom the Spirit convicts heed them as a lamp that shines in a dark place, in order that the day dawns and the morning star rises in their hearts (2 Pet 1:19).

7. Does My Evangelism Call for Unbelievers to Make a Decision?[10]

A personal evangelist does not evangelize merely to convey information about Jesus. Rather, a personal evangelist evangelizes in order to call people to saving faith in Jesus. Edward Rommen states, "Given the personal nature of the gospel, evangelism is essentially the issuing of an invitation to participate in the restoration offered by Christ."[11] He continues, "Talking about conversation instead of conversion misses the point, since the end re-

---

10 An expanded discussion of reasons for this assertion is presented in O. S. Hawkins and Matt Queen, *The Gospel Invitation: Why Publicly Inviting People to Receive Christ Still Matters* (Nashville: Thomas Nelson, 2023), 26-45.

11 Rommen, *Get Real*, 183.

sult of evangelism is an acceptance of the invitation and a radical transformation of the recipient's life."[12]

An evangelistic presentation must include a call for decision for at least two reasons. First, evangelistic presentations recorded in the New Testament include a call for unbelievers to repent of their sins and believe in Jesus Christ for their salvation (*e.g.*, Matt 3:2; 4:17; Mark 1:14-15; Acts 2:38; 3:19; 14:15; 26:20). Second, unbelievers do not know how to respond to the gospel apart from receiving instruction through an evangelistic invitation (*e.g.*, Luke 3:10-14; Acts 2:37; 16:30). A personal evangelist's aim should emulate the desire of August Hermann Francke when he wrote, "As far as I am concerned, I must preach that should someone hear me only once before he dies, he will have heard not just a part, but the entire way of salvation and in the proper way for it to take root in his heart."[13]

On the basis of these reasons, ask yourself, "Does my evangelistic proclamation incorporate an invitation to receive Christ as recorded in the New Testament?" Also ask yourself, "After I present the gospel to an unbeliever, does he know how he can receive the gospel?" In the New Testament, those who hear the gospel make a decision, whether positive or negative, in regards to what they have heard (*e.g.*, Acts 17:32-33).

The inherent nature of the gospel elicits a response on the part of those who hear it. Do you present the gospel in such a way that your hearers realize they have a decision to make? Or do they leave the conversation indifferent and unaware of their responsibility to receive the forgiveness of sins, reconcile with the Father, receive eternal life, and be indwelled by

---

12 Rommen, *Get Real*, 183.

13 Paulus Scharpff, *History of Evangelism: Three Hundred Years of Evangelism in Germany, Great Britain, and the United States of America*, Helga Bender Henry, trans. (Grand Rapids: Eerdmans, 1966), 46.

the Holy Spirit through repenting of their sins and believing in Christ for salvation?

8. Does My Evangelism Work?[14]

While a believer should evangelize with all excellence and purge ineffective practices, McCloskey has something else in mind by asking this question. He frames the intended meaning of this assessment question by offering another: "Does my philosophy and practice of evangelism make me effective in getting the gospel out to as many as possible, as soon as possible, and as clearly as possible?"[15] In other words, does what you believe about evangelism encourage or hinder your practice of it?

Permit two words of warning concerning one's beliefs and his commitment to a working—that is, an active, practice of evangelism. First, someone's merely believing in the necessity and importance of evangelism does not guarantee that he will evangelize. Second, no matter how "biblical" someone perceives his beliefs to be, any belief that deters him from evangelizing inevitably will lead him to deter others from evangelizing.

Numerous helpful campaigns, apparel, and apps exist to assist Christians in evangelizing consistently. Though space limitations prevent including all of them in this book, permit me to suggest one helpful way that encourages believers to practice consistent evangelism. Consider incorporating the following "soul-winner's prayer" in your daily prayers: "Dear Heavenly Father, give me the opportunity to share the gospel today. When it happens, help me to recognize it. When I recognize it, give me the courage to proceed [to evangelize]."

---

14 McCloskey, *Tell it Often-Tell it Well*, 186.
15 McCloskey, *Tell it Often-Tell it Well*, 186.

Although this prayer itself cannot guarantee that someone's evangelism will always "work," who can doubt that a believer's genuinely and daily asking God for (1) an opportunity to evangelize; (2) the recognition of that opportunity; and (3) the courage to act on that opportunity would not cause him to work at his evangelism?

Conclusion

What a believer thinks about evangelism influences his evangelistic practices or the lack thereof; however, what the Scriptures say about evangelism must inform and correct a believer's evangelistic practices. Though not an exhaustive list, the previous eight questions can assist a believer in evaluating his philosophy of evangelism so that he is able to ensure his passion for the Great Commission results in biblically informed, evangelistic activity.

PERSONAL REFLECTION GUIDE

1. After reflecting on the questions in this chapter, what changes, if any, should you make to the ways you approach or think about evangelism?

2. Are there additional questions, beyond those included in this chapter, that help you evaluate your own approach and mindset toward evangelism?

GROUP LEADER DISCUSSION GUIDE

TOPIC	ENGAGE THE GROUP	EXPLORE THE ISSUE	EXECUTE THE PLAN
1: Assessing Evangelism Biblically and Theologically	• Ask the group why Jesus' death, burial, and resurrection is (1) the only sacrifice that satisfies God's wrath against human sin and (2) the only provision by which unbelievers can be saved. • Ask the group to share some specific ways evangelism was practiced in the New Testament (*e.g.*, preaching; teaching; personal conversations; public defenses; public, persuasive reasoning). • Discuss with the group some factors that should motivate obedience to make baptized, obedient disciples through evangelism (*e.g.*, a love for God; a love for the lost; gratitude to God; the fear of God).	• Ask, "In what ways might our theology about salvation and evangelism influence how we share the gospel?" • Ask, "How closely do our evangelistic methods resemble those observed in the New Testament?" • Ask, "To what extent do we obey Jesus' Great Commission with urgency and faithfulness?"	• Encourage group members to evaluate and adjust their own evangelistic methods with biblical faithfulness.

TOPIC	ENGAGE THE GROUP	EXPLORE THE ISSUE	EXECUTE THE PLAN
2: Applying Evangelism Spiritually and Scripturally	• Ask group members to share one Bible verse they almost always use when evangelizing. • Ask group members to share memorable stories of times when they witnessed the Holy Spirit either (1) precede an evangelistic conversation they had with unbelievers; (2) convict sinners of their sin upon hearing the gospel; or (3) regenerate someone with whom they shared the gospel. • Ask the group how they explain repentance and faith to unbelievers when they extend a call for them to respond to the gospel.	• Ask, "How can incorporating Scripture in your gospel presentations provide clarity to your hearers and power in your evangelism?" • Ask, "Upon which do you rely more when you evangelize: (1) your experience and skill; (2) the relational familiarity you share and the trust you have with the unbeliever; or (3) the preceding, convicting, and regenerating work of the Holy Spirit?" • Have group members evaluate whether their recent gospel presentations call unbelievers to repent and believe or just present the facts of the gospel.	• Have group members suggest ways they can share gospel presentations that more faithfully involve dependency on the Holy Spirit, incorporate the Scriptures, and include invitations to repent and believe.

Chapter 9

A Strategy to Reach the Homes in Your Community with the Gospel

---

In September 2009 students, faculty, and staff at Southwestern Seminary accepted the responsibility to share the gospel with every one of the nearly 6,700 households within a one-mile radius of the seminary's campus. The initiative, called *Taking the Hill*, involved intentional, door-to-door evangelism by teams of seminary students, faculty, and staff. Ambitious though it was, the mission was completed by the end of 2010.

Southwestern Seminary then launched a follow-up effort to reach those who were not home during the initial outreach and received only a door hanger with a gospel presentation. This continued effort, called *No Soul Left Behind*, challenged students, faculty, and staff to participate in a second wave of evangelism to the surrounding community. This campaign was completed by the end of 2012.

In September 2013 the seminary expanded its evangelistic efforts to reach homes within a two-mile radius of the campus in a campaign called *Going the Second Mile*. In August 2016 the seminary's evangelistic focus advanced beyond a specific geographic area by encouraging students, faculty, and staff to share the gospel with whomever they encountered wherever they found themselves. The nomenclature, *Everyday Evangelism*, was adopted to describe this initiative. This effort endeavored to foster an expectation that the entire seminary community evangelize everyday in universities, homes, restaurants, coffee shops, parks, neighborhoods, or whatever locations the Lord would daily lead them.

By God's grace, a culture of *everyday evangelism* was created at Southwestern Seminary. For several years daily reports were made by students, faculty, and staff of their witnessing encounters' resulting in men, women, boys, and girls coming to faith in Christ. Even more incredible is the fact that between 2010 and 2018, more than 1,600 professions of faith were recorded through these daily and intentional evangelistic efforts.

Over the years, several pastors across the Southern Baptist Convention heard about these evangelistic efforts and subsequently reproduced related initiatives in their own churches. In a similar vein, I want to challenge you to motivate and mobilize your congregation to reach every home within a one-mile radius of your church's campus. This suggestion is not based on a belief that door-to-door evangelism is the *only* way to evangelize. It is not. Nevertheless, I might also add that door-to-door evangelism is not the *only* way *not* to evangelize.

Door-to-door evangelism does, however, provide at least three notable benefits to churches that practice it. First, as my seminary evangelism professor opined regarding door-to-door evangelism, "If you visit those you do not reach, you will reach those you do not visit." Second, I know of no other more intentional way to reach your community than to visit the homes of those who live in it. Last, both the number of repetitions and the variety of conversations resulting from door-to-door visits provide members of your church with the kind of real-world practice and hands-on experience in evangelism that both encourages and prepares them to evangelize on their own.

Making and executing a plan to reach every house in a given area with the gospel seems daunting, but with the proper planning and preparation, it is not impossible. This chapter is not meant to be an exhaustive explanation of how to plan and execute such an initiative, but it does reflect some helpful lessons learned and implemented in the aforementioned evangelistic campaigns. My prayer is that you will take this primer and make it work in your context. Since every community is different, your strategy should take into account the strengths and weaknesses of your church and the uniqueness of your community.

STEPS FOR REACHING YOUR COMMUNITY

1. Pray for a Brokenhearted Congregation

No mighty movement will occur within a community until church members' hearts are spiritually broken and burdened for their neighbors. Before you pray for direction in executing an evangelism plan, you must begin by praying for the hearts of your church members. If the Lord is going to move in a mighty way, He is going to do it through the mobilization of the people in your pews. A pastor or church member can lead such an endeavor, but he cannot accomplish it by himself.

Begin by asking God's Spirit to move within the hearts of your fellow church members. Petition Him to raise up leaders and motivators who will encourage the people in your church to become active in reaching your community for Christ. While you hope that every member of your church will immediately join the effort and participate, this virtuous desire will likely not become a reality right away. Remember, Jesus began the work of His evangelistic enterprise with only twelve (*cf.*, Matt 10:1-4; Luke 6:12-16) untrained and ordinary men (*cf.*, Acts 4:13).

To begin, you simply need a core group of believers committed to the goal. Therefore, cast your evangelistic vision broadly throughout your church and utilize those whom God gives you to start reaching the lost. Over time, the fruits of your initial evangelistic efforts will serve to inspire and encourage other church members to join you in reaching your community for Christ.

2. Know Your Community and Your Church

This suggestion sounds elementary, but it is critical to develop an evangelistic strategy compatible with the people you intend to reach with the gospel. Every pastor should understand his community—the uniqueness of its people, its culture(s), and how its people interact with one another. Some pertinent considerations will come to mind intuitively. When can you find most people to be at home? Obviously, you will want to take this into consideration in order to reach the maximum number of people. Daytime Monday through Friday may work magnificently for one area but terribly for another. Saturdays might prove an ideal time for part of the year, but if a high population of young children resides in your community, they and their families will likely be at ballgames instead of their homes on weekends. Every community is unique, so realistically consider the unique profile of your community.

You must also know your community statistically. How many homes are within one mile of your church? Two miles? Three miles? How many people do those homes represent? If you cannot answer these questions based on census or other concrete data, then you will possess inadequate and incomplete information to formulate your evangelistic strategy. Data of this nature will both inform and form the foundation of your outreach.

One of the best ways to find this information is to visit the North American Missions Board's (NAMB) website and complete a demographic graphic request (*https://www.namb.net/contact/demographics-request*). There you will enter your church's address, set different radii to determine the number of homes around your church, and acquire additional data about your community. This report will provide you with an accurate picture of your community's size and demographics. If your community has experienced a significant population boom or decline in the last three to five years, you might consider visiting your city's governmental agencies, such as the tax assessor or the zoning commission, for more up-to-date information.

Finally, you must know your church. When are the best times for church members to make evangelistic visits? You want to maximize the number of people who are available to go door-to-door. There may be multiple times throughout the week when different groups can visit. The key to scheduling outreach events and activities will be flexibility and adjustment. Do not be afraid to try several different times in order to learn the most ideal times for those who want to participate to do so. Ultimately, having a smaller group of your members energized from regularly finding people at home with whom they can talk about Jesus will provide more momentum in the mobilization of your congregation to evangelize than a large group of members who become discouraged because they weekly fail to find anyone home with whom they can share the gospel.

Helpful Hints:

» Part of knowing your community is knowing potential dangers in your community. Are there areas that you should not visit after certain times? Are there areas to which you should not send certain groups because the area is unsafe? Your local police department should be willing to help you identify these areas and times, and in many cases online resources can pinpoint the locations of committed crimes within a given period of time.

» Additionally, it is imperative that you research all known criminals, especially sex offenders, in your area and put them on a separate list before you begin sending your people to visit homes. The pastor and a deacon or another church leader should visit these homes in order to ensure the safety of everyone involved. Registry information for sex offense criminals is available at *https://www.nsopw.gov.*

3. Set Your Scope

Southwestern Seminary began its first evangelistic campaign by setting a one-mile radius around its campus. A one-mile radius may be too large an area for churches in densely populated communities because it could conceivably take years to visit that number of houses; however, churches located in rural areas may have to expand their radii to five miles because there may only be five hundred homes within five miles of their campus. Setting the scope is an essential process that requires much prayer. If you set your scope too large or wide, you risk setting a goal that overwhelms your members so that they quit before the vision is realized.

What, therefore, is a reasonable goal to set? For starters, you could choose an area that would reasonably take your congregation twelve to twenty-four months to visit each home in the selected area. Calculate the number of people you anticipate participating, along with the interval of time it will take them to visit each home. Many churches will have teams visiting only one day a week for one hour at a time, so you want to give them an assigned number of houses that is reasonably reached within that timeframe. On average an evangelism team will visit five houses within an hour.

Once you have determined how many homes a team can reasonably visit in an hour, you need to gauge how many church members you expect to participate regularly. Using the base number of five houses per team with twenty people participating weekly translates into ten teams of two visiting approximately fifty homes per week. If your church can maintain that number for forty weeks in a year, it will reach 2,000 homes annually. Over an eighteen-month period, your church would visit roughly 3,000 homes for its campaign. Obviously, you will have to adjust your number based upon the number of participants in your congregation, but the hope is that the longer you evangelize, the more energized and committed your people become about it.

Once the scope has been set, you can then work on collecting addresses for your area. The most comprehensive and intuitive tool to assist your church with assembling addresses and generating team assignments is *EvangeGo* (*https://www.evangego.com*).

Apart from subscribing to this service, you will have to conduct your own research in order to accumulate addresses for team assignments. If you decide not to utilize *EvangeGo*, some other suggestions whereby you might obtain addresses include consulting your local electricity company, tax assessor's office, office of public records, and/or public library. Because the ways and repositories to access residential information manually varies and requires numerous manhours to complete, enlist church members to assist you.

4. Plan and Track Your Follow-Up Efforts

Before making home visits, you and your church must ask yourselves some crucial, logistical questions in order to maximize the church's efforts. For example, how will the church follow-up if someone surrenders his life to Christ? What action will be taken concerning someone who is seriously seeking the Lord but is not ready to receive Him during the visit? You and your church must organize and establish a follow-up plan in order to (1) assimilate new believers into the church membership; (2) mature them to live in the Spirit and obey the Word; and (3) mobilize them to make disciples.

To aid in follow-up efforts, evangelism teams must complete simple reports detailing important notes about their visits (such as whether the team spoke to someone at the house, how the individual responded to the gospel, particular insights arising out of the conversation, prayer requests, etc.). The data from these reports should then be transferred to a database for follow-up. Thus, an organized reporting process makes your church's efforts more efficient and effective. Someone in your church might not be able to visit homes on a regular basis, but he can commit forty-five minutes per week to catalog all of the reports into *EvangeGo*, an Excel spreadsheet, or a Google sheet. Such a commitment will greatly assist the pastor and follow-up teams to be mobilized for a prompt response to new believers' decisions and unbelievers' needs.

Helpful Hints:

> »   Follow-up sooner rather than later. Do not let more than a week pass before you follow-up with someone who needs additional care.
> »   Encourage the person who made the initial contact to be involved in the follow-up efforts.

5. Train, Resource, And Mobilize Your People

If your church actively evangelizes, then you likely have an existing process whereby members are equipped to share Christ. If, however, this kind of endeavor is new to the church, then members would benefit from evangelism training prior to being deployed into the community. Such preparation should help them overcome fears associated with evangelism.

Most Christians understand the gospel and can generally express its major tenets. However, they often lack the confidence or a framework to articulate it to unbelievers. Some tools that equip members in evangelism include *Evangelizing without Memorizing*,[1] *Getting to the Gospel*,[2] *Three Circles*, *The Romans Road*, and *One-Verse Evangelism*. Whatever method(s) you choose to utilize, be consistent, and train people so that they feel confident. Encouraging members to share the gospel with one another during a training session might feel awkward to them, but after they have had a few repetitions, they will feel much more comfortable when they stand on the doorstep of a complete stranger. Once church members are equipped to share the gospel effectively,

---

1 This video training is available at *https://www.bit.ly/evangelizingwithoutmemorizing*; accessed on August 3, 2025.

2 This video training is available at *https://www.bit.ly/gettingtothegospel*; accessed on August 3, 2025.

they need clear, organized directions on how to accomplish the goal. Thoughtful planning and organization make the process more enjoyable, efficient, and rewarding.

Southwestern created Assignment Reports for teams to use (see the Sample on the next page).[3] Each Report included the addresses for five homes as well as enough space to record important information regarding each visit. They were numbered in case one was lost or misplaced.

When teams were deployed into the neighborhoods, they signed out an assignment sheet and then signed it back in when they returned. This process helped data entry volunteers to track where the teams were going and who was responsible to return the form(s). On some occasions, the same report was checked out three times because a team had an hour-long conversation with one person so that it could not visit the remaining houses. The goal of this process was to ensure that none of the unvisited homes were overlooked and not visited.

Additionally, because each report noted the team members who visited each home, when a data entry volunteer had questions about a visit or notation made on the assignment sheet, then he could contact a team member to get clarity or answers to his questions.

One primary aim with any assignment report is simplicity. By answering "Yes/No" questions about the visit, you are able to distill the visit information to a manageable size. If teams were required to include everything that either occurred or was learned during the course of a visit, it would require hours to process the results of the visit. A streamlined report assists in gathering

---

3 You and/or your church have permission to re-create and generate reports like the sample provided. However, an advantageous benefit of the *EvangeGo* tool is that it automatically and effortlessly generates Assignment Reports of the homes that are selected to be visited.

Sample of an Assignment Report

Assignment: Quadrant 3 - Map 1

11 BRYSON CIRCLE, 11111

Date: _____

Name: _____

Phone: _____

E-mail: _____

(Please write details of visit on the back of this form.)

Was anyone home? ☐ Yes ☐ No

Was the Gospel presented" ☐ Yes ☐ No

Were there professions of faith? ☐ Yes ☐ No

If yes, collect contact info for follow-up:

Names: _____

Phone: _____ Language Spoken: _____

12 BRYSON CIRCLE, 11111

Date: _____

Name: _____

Phone: _____

E-mail: _____

(Please write details of visit on the back of this form.)

Was anyone home? ☐ Yes ☐ No

Was the Gospel presented? ☐ Yes ☐No

Were there professions of faith? ☐ Yes ☐ No

If yes, collect contact info for follow-up:

Names: _____

Phone: _____ Language Spoken: _____

13 BRYSON CIRCLE, 11111

Date: _____

Name: _____

Phone: _____

E-mail: _____

(Please write details of visit on the back of this form.)

Was anyone home? ☐ Yes ☐ No

Was the Gospel presented? ☐ Yes ☐ No

Were there professions of faith? ☐ Yes ☐ No

If yes, collect contact info for follow-up:

Names: _____

Phone: _____ Language Spoken: _____

14 BRYSON CIRCLE, 11111

Date: _____

Name: _____

Phone: _____

E-mail: _____

(Please write details of visit on the back of this form.)

Was anyone home? ☐ Yes ☐ No

Was the Gospel presented? ☐ Yes ☐ No

Were there professions of faith? ☐ Yes ☐ No

If yes, collect contact info for follow-up:

Names: _____

Phone: _____ Language Spoken: _____

15 BRYSON CIRCLE, 11111

Date: _____

Name: _____

Phone: _____

E-mail: _____

(Please write details of visit on the back of this form.)

Was anyone home? ☐ Yes ☐ No

Was the Gospel presented? ☐ Yes ☐ No

Were there professions of faith? ☐ Yes ☐No

If yes, collect contact info for follow-up:

Names: _____

Phone: _____ Language Spoken: _____

PLEASE RETURN THIS FORM TO THE PASTOR.

necessary information that can be entered easily into *EvangeGo*, an Excel spreadsheet, or a Google sheet and be tracked for later follow-up. Stress to teams the importance of filling in all the required information.

In addition to an assignment report, teams should be equipped with resources to share the gospel. Some helpful tools to accompany each team's assignment report include informational door hangers and/or gospel tracts that faithfully and clearly present the gospel in the majority language spoken by community members, as well as one or two Bibles or New Testaments. If no one answers the door, the team should leave the door hanger. If a team engages the homeowner in a brief conversation, it should leave a tract. If an extended spiritual conversation ensues and the person shows interest in or receives the gospel, the team should provide him with a Bible. Encourage evangelism teams to end each visit with a brief prayer for needs or requests of the homeowner(s).

6. Encourage Your People Continually

If you envision that your church's evangelistic initiative will take a year or two to complete, the members need to see progress and hear reports of encouragement along the way; otherwise, they may become disinterested or discouraged. Develop a way to lead the church to celebrate corporately as well as to be informed about the overall progress of the effort. Some suggestions include: (1) brief praise reports of positive witnessing encounters; (2) testimonies by those who have become new disciples during evangelistic visits; (3) a colored ping-pong ball display that indicates the weekly number of (a) church members who have committed to pray for an unbelieving friend or family member, (b) church members who have presented the gospel, (c) new believers who have professed their faith in Christ, and (d) new believers who have been baptized; and/or (4) corporate prayer for teams' weekly visits. Publicly communicating to the congregation in these ways demonstrates the progress it has made towards the goal as well as ways God is moving in and through the church.

Helpful Hints:

>> When a church member sees someone come to faith, have him write a brief email describing the conversation, and include it in a weekly email newsletter to be sent to church members.

>> Invite people to give testimonies during services about what God did when they visited.

>> Print a large map of your radius, post it in a prominent place in the church, and shade the areas you have visited. Ask church members to pray that the gospel witness shared with the residents who live in those specific areas will take effect.

PERSONAL REFLECTION GUIDE

1. **Does your church have an intentional strategy to reach the households in your community?**
   >> If so, can any of the suggestions in this chapter strengthen it?
   >> If not, how might you suggest either this chapter's strategy or another to your pastor and the leadership of your church?
2. **What can you do to inspire and encourage your church—as an encouraging evangelism cata-**

lyst—to reach the homes and families in your community with the gospel?

GROUP LEADER DISCUSSION GUIDE

TOPIC	ENGAGE THE GROUP	EXPLORE THE ISSUE	EXECUTE THE PLAN
1: Church Strategy for Community Outreach	• Ask the group, "What is our church's strategic plan to reach households in our community with the gospel?"	• If a plan exists, ask, "How can the strategies suggested in this chapter improve or complement our existing outreach efforts?" • If no plan exists, ask, "What obstacles or challenges, such as fear, apathy, and/or lack of knowledge, might be preventing our church from having such a plan?"	• As a group, develop a clear, actionable plan for how you will present this chapter's strategy (or any alternative ideas that emerged in discussion) to your pastor(s) and church leadership, with the goal of inviting them to partner with you in implementing it.

TOPIC	ENGAGE THE GROUP	EXPLORE THE ISSUE	EXECUTE THE PLAN
2: Inspiring and Encouraging Evangelism within the Church	• Ask the group, "In what specific ways can we encourage one another, as well as inspire the church as a whole, to engage families and homes in the community with the gospel?"	• Ask, "What specific actions and/or attitudes can foster a culture of evangelism and encouragement within our church?" • If the church and/or its leadership seem opposed to adopting a community evangelism strategy, ask, "How can we lovingly and patiently address and overcome the barrier(s) we previously identified in **Topic 1: Church Strategy for Community Outreach**?"	• Have the group pray for God to grant openness and vision to the pastor(s) and the leadership to adopt or strengthen the church's outreach plans.

www.ingramcontent.com/pod-product-compliance
Lightning Source LLC
Chambersburg PA
CBHW020739130626
46554CB00006B/2058